A Bigger Picture
Viewing the World Through God's Eyes

Danny B. Powell

Isaiah 61 One Publishing
https://isaiah61onepublishing.com

DEDICATION

For my children, Zachry, Cheyenne, Olivia, and Sophia. Your relationship with God is unique to you, but I wanted to share with you my struggles and thoughts. My story is your legacy. To know how a man thinks, read what he writes.

DEDICATION i

ACKNOWLEDGMENTS iii

Chapter One To Bake Or Not to Bake 1

Chapter Two What Is Love? 12

Chapter Three The Lord's Name In Vain 19

Chapter Four Trading Truth For A Lie 27

Chapter Five Acceptable Sins 33

Chapter Six Good Bye To Religion 43

Chapter Seven Thursday Night 51

Chapter Eight Learning to Pray 60

Chapter Nine How Much Are You Worth? 66

Chapter Ten Discovering God 74

Chapter Eleven Hiding From God 80

Chapter Twelve I Have To Be Poor? 88

Chapter Thirteen The Most Toys WINS! 96

Chapter Fourteen Hosea 102

Chapter Fifteen Stealing My Joy 115

Chapter Sixteen A Drink Of Water 121

Chapter Eighteen Meeting Jesus Christ 133

ABOUT THE AUTHOR 139

ACKNOWLEDGMENTS

I am humbled that anyone would care what I think about anything. Multiple people have encouraged me over the last couple of decades to put my observations and thoughts into book form. Among those that encouraged me are my wife, Rachel, and Pastor Cindy Hyde whose very presence encourages everyone she encounters. Without them, this project would never have gotten out of my mind onto paper (or e-Reader). I'd also like to thank Mary Ann Naranjo for "making me" put together the annual company cookbook when I worked for her and her husband, Neal Naranjo. She was a ruthless editor that made me understand why it was important to be consistent throughout the book. Those lessons saved immeasurable time creating this book. I have to mention Harley Schnell, who gave me the title for this book, but no, Harley, you are not getting royalties! Also, as you read my thoughts, you'll discover that I use modern conversational English. I was horrified that because of copyright reasons I was going to have to use the King James Version of the Bible for my quotes. Nothing "wrong" with the KJV, it was good enough for the Apostle Paul to read to baby Jesus in the manger, so it's good enough for me, but I want to thank the World English Bible for publishing a public domain modern translation of the American Standard Version.

Chapter One
To Bake Or Not to Bake

If I were a professional baker, would I bake the cake for the gay couple that just came into my shop and asked me to make for their wedding? A post on Facebook by my friend Rebekah triggered this question in my mind. In her post, she posted a meme asking: "Confused about the 'Christian Response' to social issues? Here's a handy reference list." Then there is a list of groups of people: male, female, unsure, gay, straight, unsure, addict, sober, believer, unbeliever, and unsure. The answer for every group of people is "love them." That answer, "love them," seemed reasonable enough to me when I first encountered the meme. When asked, Jesus said that the most important commandment is love:

> "Jesus said to him, "'You shall love the Lord your God with all your heart, with all your soul, and with all your mind.' This is the first and great commandment. A second likewise is this, 'You shall love your neighbor as yourself.' The whole law and the prophets depend on these two commandments." (Matthew 22:37-40)

In another place in Scripture He says:

> "A new commandment I give to you, that you love one another. Just as I have loved you, you also love one another. By this everyone will know that you are my disciples if you have love for one another." (John 13:34-35)

Imagine my bewilderment while many of Rebekah and I's mutual friends and people I consider brothers and sisters in Christ roasted Rebekah for even posting such a thing! Not only was Rebekah being roasted, but many of the people commenting were attacking one another. Hardly the love we are to show for each other as Christ commanded us.

Of all the groups listed on the meme, the group that got the most response are gays and lesbians. Homosexuality has a special place of hatred in modern Christianity. I find that interesting because in at least one place in the Bible, homosexuality and slander (or gossip) are on equal footing.

> "Or don't you know that the unrighteous will not inherit God's Kingdom? Don't be deceived. Neither the sexually immoral, nor idolaters, nor adulterers, nor male prostitutes, nor homosexuals, nor thieves, nor covetous, nor drunkards, nor slanderers, nor extortionists, will inherit God's Kingdom." (1 Corinthians 6:9-10)

There is also some confusion about what "love" is and how that ought to govern our actions towards other human beings. Here is the very first post in response to the meme:

> Biblical Love can't exist if you continue to let unrepentant sinners sin without speaking to them about the sin and the result of being sinful (Hell) as well as giving one's life to Christ.
>
> Human love says "Do what you want; I'll love you."
>
> Christ-like Love says:" I Love you but what you're doing is wrong and I'm concerned for you and your soul."

As I read that first comment, I immediately thought of the guy standing on the corner with a bullhorn yelling at everyone that walks by to TURN OR BURN! I see those people every year at the local Fourth of July Festival standing on the bridge leading to the park yelling at everyone. Most everyone is walking by ignoring them except for some that want to argue with them and shout back at them. I am amused and will walk a little slower, so I can hear some of the discussion. Some will argue attempting to debate Scripture and others will mainly want to tell them where they can go! Everyone is yelling, no one is listening, and no one changes their mind. What kind of love is that?

The second thought I had was something one of my pastors stated years ago regarding protesting in front of abortion clinics. He said he refused to participate in an abortion protest. It wasn't because he supported the practice, he said it is because the people going into the clinics are our mission. How can he expect a young woman that's hurting and remorseful to listen to anything he might have to offer when she already feels judged and condemned because she saw him at a protest?

Phillip Yancey writes in his book, What's So Amazing About Grace, about a prostitute he invited to church:

> "Church! Why would I ever go there? I was already feeling terrible about myself. They'd make me feel worse."1

In that first comment to Rebekah's meme, I noticed that there are three different kinds of love mentioned: biblical, human, and Christ-like. A different definition follows each of those three. In the Scriptures, I quoted earlier Jesus says "love." I wonder what kind of love Jesus meant? Did He mean any of those three or does He mean something entirely different?

---

1 Philip Yancey, What's So Amazing About Grace, page 11, © 1997 Zondervan,

One thing I noticed about all three types of love listed in that post was they all three seem to indicate that how one loves is related to the state of a relationship. That is something I must incorporate into this process. In my question, the couple walking into my bakery are strangers to me. Before the couple came into my business, I had no relationship with them. Does this fact work into the type of love I extend to these human beings? Are there, in fact, different types of love? How many more?

Reading through the New Testament, I read lots of times where Messiah interacted with publicly known sinners. There is the story of the woman caught in the very act of adultery:

> "Now very early in the morning, he came again into the temple, and all the people came to him. He sat down and taught them. The scribes and the Pharisees brought a woman taken in adultery. Having set her in the middle, they told him, "Teacher, we found this woman in adultery, in the very act. Now in our law, Moses commanded us to stone such women. What then do you say about her?" They said this, testing him, that they might have something to accuse him of. But Jesus stooped down and wrote on the ground with his finger. But when they continued asking him, he looked up and said to them, "He who is without sin among you, let him throw the first stone at her." Again, he stooped down, and with his finger wrote on the ground. They, when they heard it, being convicted by their conscience, went out one by one, beginning from the oldest, even to the last. Jesus was left alone with the woman where she was, in the middle. Jesus, standing up, saw her and said, "Woman, where are your accusers? Did no one condemn you?" She said, "No one, Lord." Jesus said, "Neither do I condemn you. Go your way. From now on, sin no more." (John 8:2-11)

Those scribes and Pharisees were well within their rights under the Law of Moses to stone that woman. They were doing what they believed to be the right thing. The Scripture doesn't imply or infer that she didn't commit adultery. From the text, it is clear that she indeed committed adultery. Jesus, called Teacher in this translation, Rabbi in others, should have joined those condemning the woman. But instead, His response is not what anyone would have reasonably expected. Rather than joining them, He does something entirely unexpected. He starts writing on the ground with His finger. The Scriptures don't record what Jesus was writing in the sand. A favorite story the Rabbis often teach is that He was writing the individual sins of people in the crowd for everyone to see. We can only speculate what He was writing. However, the end of this story is the interesting thing: "where have your accusers gone? ... then neither will I". Christ Jesus, Son of God, Lord of the Universe, the ONE person qualified to judge or condemn this woman, told this sinner that He neither accuses nor condemns her. Yes, He did tell her to "go and sin no more," but that isn't how He started the interaction with her. *First He saved her.*

What about this story of Jesus hanging out with sinners?

> "After these things he went out and saw a tax collector named Levi sitting at the tax office, and said to him, "Follow me!" He left everything and rose up and followed him. Levi made a great feast for him in his house. There was a great crowd of tax collectors and others who were reclining with them. Their scribes and the Pharisees murmured against his disciples, saying, "Why do you eat and drink with the tax collectors and sinners?" Jesus answered them, "Those who are healthy do not need a physician, but those who are sick do. I have not come to call the righteous, but sinners to repentance." (Luke 5:27-32)

Tax collectors were one of the most hated groups of people amongst the Jews. They were considered traitors, thieves, and extortionists. The reasons were the tax collectors were Jews that collaborated with Rome to collect the tax money that paid for Rome to rule over them and because tax collectors were also known for extracting more tax than was due padding their own pockets. Jesus dared to dine with them! Imagine that! What would His reaction to this situation be today? Would Jesus go and dine with a different group that is hated by people now? Would Jesus eat dinner with a traitor or extortionist?

In the New Testament, I cannot find any example of Jesus telling someone other than the ultra-religious that they needed to clean up before they could approach Him or before He could approach them. Always, Jesus meets a need before He tells them to sin no more.

One of my wife's favorite Bible stories is about a man with leprosy. Leprosy is a contagious disease that affects the skin, mucous membranes, and nerves, causing discoloration and lumps on the skin and, in severe cases, disfigurement and deformities. While rare in modern times, it was prevalent in Biblical times and there is an entire set of laws and regulations regarding how to act if one has the disease and how one should act around someone with it. People with leprosy were considered "unclean" and "untouchable." Banished to outside the gates of the city, if someone with leprosy saw someone coming towards them, they had to declare, "Unclean! Unclean!" This warned people coming towards them would move away and avoid contact. If one came into contact with a leper, that person would then be ceremoniously "unclean." A prevailing thought is that leprosy was some punishment for sin, so by default, a leper would be considered a sinner. One time some disciples asked Jesus about a man's infirmary.

> "His disciples asked him, "Rabbi, who sinned, this man or his parents, that he was born blind?" (John 9:2)

The conventional thinking then and by many now is that disease or deformity is punishment for sin. However, this is how the Lord answered the question:

> "Jesus answered, "Neither did this man sin, nor his parents; but, that the works of God might be revealed in him." (John 9:3)

Death and disease and imperfection are the results of sin, not the punishment for it. Paul writes in Romans that the "wages of sin are death" (Romans 6:23). God told Adam in Eden, "…on the day you eat of it (the fruit from the tree of the knowledge of good and evil), you will surely die." (Genesis 2:17) The punishment is death, not sickness or misfortune.

Rachel likes this story because when she shares her testimony, she states that she too was a leper. She relates to being considered unclean and untouchable. She starts in Luke:

> "While he was in one of the cities, behold, there was a man full of leprosy. When he saw Jesus, he fell on his face, and begged him, saying, "Lord, if you want to, you can make me clean." He stretched out his hand, and touched him, saying, "I want to. Be made clean." Immediately leprosy left him." (Luke 5:12-13)

When Rachel tells this story, she says that she doesn't think our Lord simply stretched out His hand and lightly touched the leper. She believes, and if you heard her tell this story, you'd believe it too, that He reached out His hand and took the man's face into His hands, that He caressed the man's face. The leper probably had had no human contact in a very long time. By the laws the scribes and Pharisees developed to ensure Israel would always be in alignment with the 10 Commandments, Jesus, by touching the leper, was now "unclean" and could not go back into the city without first going to a priest and performing some ritual (which, in the next two verses in Luke He instructs the leper to do).

Rachel continues telling her story regarding this passage of Scripture:

> "Jesus touched me. My epiphany came when I realized that Jesus, too, became a leper. The Bible says:
>
> For our sake he made him to be sin who knew no sin so that in Him we might become the righteousness of God. (2 Corinthians 5:21 ESV)
>
> Whipped and flogged, and finally nailed to a cross. Jesus knows the pain I felt and then some. He did it for me. He did it for you. I tell people to beware of saviors that don't bear scars. Jesus bears yours and my scars. Lepers were "the untouchables." Jesus became untouchable, just like I was. Knowing this changed me drastically."

When Rachel describes Jesus touching her, she describes it in an authentic, physical way. The question becomes: "Would Jesus touch a sinner today?"

Some religious leaders considered Jesus, a sinner because of the company He kept:

> "The Son of Man came eating and drinking, and they say, 'Behold, a gluttonous man, and a drunkard, a friend of tax collectors and sinners!' But wisdom is justified by her children." (Matthew 11:19)

They called Jesus a sinner! Shocking news because we know from Scripture that He was without sin. My thinking is they called Jesus a sinner not because He was, but because He didn't act the way the religious leaders thought He ought to behave. I don't know what kind of sinners you've dealt with, but I have a hard time believing sinners would have wanted to be around Jesus if He was telling them to turn or burn before He could join them.

A favorite lyric of mine is from a Casting Crowns song, "God's gotta change her heart before He changes her shirt."2 We claim Jesus meets us where we are. Why do we expect more from others than God expects from us? The most cited Bible verse is John 3:16. When it says God so loves the WORLD, does that include sinners? If not, is there hope for any of us?

Back to Rebekah's Facebook post. In response to the very first response, another wrote:

> Wasn't it Christ Himself who loved those who were different? I'm pretty sure there are no asterisks after "love thy neighbor."

In addition to discovering what love is, we must figure out who our neighbors are. Who beyond the people living in our neighborhood are our neighbors? The best explanation is this parable Jesus told:

> "Behold, a certain lawyer stood up and tested him, saying, "Teacher, what shall I do to inherit eternal life?" He said to him, "What is written in the law? How do you read it?" He answered, "You shall love the Lord your God with all your heart, with all your soul, with all your strength, and with all your mind; and your neighbor as yourself." He said to him, "You have answered correctly. Do this, and you will live." But he, desiring to justify himself, asked Jesus, "Who is my neighbor?" Jesus answered, "A certain man was going down from Jerusalem to Jericho, and he fell among robbers, who both stripped him and beat him, and departed, leaving him half dead. By chance, a certain priest was going down that way. When he saw him, he

2 Hector Alonzo Cervantes / John Mark Hall. What the World Needs. © Sony/ATV Music Publishing LLC, Essential Music Publishing, Capitol Christian Music Group

passed by on the other side. In the same way, a Levite also, when he came to the place and saw him, passed by on the other side. But a certain Samaritan, as he traveled, came where he was. When he saw him, he was moved with compassion, came to him, and bound up his wounds, pouring on oil and wine. He set him on his animal, and brought him to an inn, and took care of him. On the next day, when he departed, he took out two denarii, and gave them to the host, and said to him, 'Take care of him. Whatever you spend beyond that, I will repay you when I return.' Now, which of these three do you think seemed to be a neighbor to him who fell among the robbers?" He said, "He who showed mercy on him." Then Jesus said to him, "Go and do likewise." (Luke 10:25-37)

This parable was particularly stinging to the Jew. Samaritans were considered lower than dogs. They were half Jew-half gentile, the result of the Assyrian conquest of northern Israel pressing the Hebrews into captivity and leaving others behind to intermarry with their Assyrian masters. They had their own Torah, religious system, and holy places. Neither Jews nor Samaritans would have anything to do with each other, yet, here is Jesus, a Jew, telling another Jew that a Samaritan, a member of a race of people that person probably abhors, is his neighbor.

That wasn't the only time Jesus referred to people we wouldn't consider our neighbors included in "love your neighbor."

"You have heard that it was said, 'You shall love your neighbor and hate your enemy.' But I tell you, love your enemies, bless those who curse you, do good to those who hate you, and pray for those who mistreat you and persecute you, that you may be children of your Father who is in heaven. For he makes his sun to rise on the evil and the good and sends rain on the just and the unjust. For if you love those who love you, what reward do you have? Don't even the tax collectors do the same?" (Matthew 5:43-46)

"...bless those who curse you, do good to those who hate you, and pray for those who mistreat you and persecute you," Does this apply to anti-Christian ultra-left wingers that want to remove God from every aspect of civilization? Does Jesus expect me to pray for, bless, and do good for them that go against Him or His word?

From what would Jesus do? We must go to how we, the born-again believer should treat sinners. Do we treat them differently than our Lord did? How are we to engage people outside the gate?

I am a born-again believer in Christ Jesus. He is my Lord. Whether to bake or not bake the wedding cake for a same-sex couple is crucial for me to consider. How does my Lord and God expect me to act?

Chapter Two
What Is Love?

What is love? When someone tells you that they love you, what does that person mean? What response is that person expecting? How does that person feel or react when they don't get that expected response? Relationships are damaged and sometimes ruined when one person tells another person that they love them and the other person doesn't respond in kind.

I had this happen at church one time. Someone I was talking to suddenly said, "I love you," to me as I was leaving. I smiled thinking how odd that was and tried to move on. As I walked away, she said it again, albeit a little louder, "I love you!" I just smiled and continued walking. She was having no part of that. She came after me, grabbed my arm, swung me around to face her, "don't you love me too?"

That got me to thinking about the subject of "love." What exactly is it? Isn't that the age-old question? Do I love this woman that just told me she loved me? What did she mean when she said she loved me? Should my wife be worried? Did she mean something else? Hundreds of thousands and maybe more poems, songs, books, movies, and art through the ages have attempted to define love. The Beatles sang "All You Need Is Love" in an odd time signature (5/4). After all these eons exploring the subject, why am I still wondering what it is? Am I capable of truly loving someone else? What about that unconditional love the Bible speaks about describing how God relates about us? Can any human love unconditionally? If humans cannot, and love is conditional, can it truly be love?

Unlike English, where "love" has multiple meanings, in Ancient Greek, the language of the New Testament, there are four different words translated *love* in English, each with precise meanings:

Éros (ἔρως érōs) meaning "love, mostly of the sexual passion,"
Philia (φιλία philía) meaning "affectionate regard, friendship," usually "between equals,"
Storge (στοργή storgē) meaning "love, affection" and "especially of parents and children," and
Agápe (ἀγάπη agápē) meaning "love: esp. charity; the love of God for man and of man for God."[3]

The New Testament uses two of these Ancient Greek words, *philia* and *agápe*. I was surprised that *storge* wasn't used even once since the relationship between God and man is often described in terms of a family with God as Father and believers as sons (or daughters). The Apostle Paul writes at least five different times in the Scriptures of believers being "sons of God."[4] Jesus instructed His followers to address God as Father[5]. In the Book of John believers are referred to as "sons of God" multiple times and in the Book of Revelation Jesus calls those who endure "sons."

The other word for love not used, *Éros*, was shocking to me because with all the emphasis Christians put on sex and because this Ancient Greek word is the source of our English word erotica, I would expect it to be mentioned at least once even if in a negative sense. My understanding is that by the time the New Testament was being written that *Éros* had become so distasteful that the writers wouldn't use it. It had become an expletive. Still, I don't understand why the Scriptures don't even mention it.

---

3 ἀγάπη, Henry George Liddell, Robert Scott, A Greek-English Lexicon, on Perseus
4 Romans 8:16; Romans 9:6-8; 2 Corinthians 6:14-18; Galatians 3:24-29; Philippians 2:15
5 Luke 11:2 and Matthew 6:9

I was further astonished to learn that in the actual definition of *agápe* it reads not only does it describe God's love for man, but it also describes how man is supposed to love God! I was already wondering if I could love the way God loves me, and then I learn the very word used to describe that love is supposed to explain how I'm supposed to love God. God loves me so much He died for me. I realize that there are martyrs around the world that die daily because of their love for God, but at the end of the day, I'm not sure I'd do the same for Him. I pray I never have to find out.

My understanding of *agápe* is that it's a *self-sacrificing-no-matter-what kind of love that is not dependent upon the reciprocation of that love from another.* To date, this kind of love is outside of my own human experience. It's easy to love someone when it benefits me in some way. My four-year-old daughter will tell me I don't love her if I don't give her what she wants. Unfortunately, I fear my understanding of love isn't much more sophisticated than hers. If I am capable of agape how do I explain where the Bible reads:

We love Him because He first loved us. (1 John 4:19 NKJV)

That verse in and of itself would seem to validate my experience thus far that I can only love someone that gives me some benefit and that my love for God is conditional upon His loving me first. Love is now something to trade, to barter, or the result of some other commerce transaction. You love me, and I'll love you back.

I quoted Jesus in Chapter 1 teaching us to love our enemies. In the Sermon on the Mount, Jesus uses the word, *agapao* (a variation of *agape*), to describe how we are to love our enemies. He teaches us to have a *self-sacrificing-no-matter-what kind of love that is not dependent upon the reciprocation of that love from another* towards our enemies! Am I even capable of doing that? To love someone that hates me and wishes me harm? Is this an example of my ideology meeting my reality?

How about considering what the most prolific writer of the New Testament, the one that defines love writes:

"For I know that in me, that is, in my flesh, dwells no good thing. For desire is present with me, but I don't find it doing that which is good." (Romans 7:18)

The "it" Paul writes about is his flesh. Paul was writing specifically about how arduous it is to do what the Lord asks us to do. If the Apostle Paul had such a difficult time doing what is good, what hope do I have?

A popular call and response I hear in church often is "God is good" to which the congregation replies, "All the time" and then the preacher says, "All the time," and the response is "God is good!" 1 John 4:16 says that "God is love." It's quite simple and uncomplicated to believe that GOD can love everyone. He's good all the time! It's what He does, right? But, how can I love to the degree that God does when there is "no good in me"?

Back to my original question, "What is love?" What exactly is *agápe*? *Agápe* can't possibly be an emotion. It can't be a warm feeling we get about someone, that most certainly would be *eros*. While sometimes love makes us feel good or happy, other times love breaks our heart, makes us despondent and sometimes drives us into the depths of despair. The emotions and feelings we associate with love are the results of love, not love itself.

The New Testament talks about two kinds of love, agape, the *self-sacrificing-no-matter-what kind of love that is not dependent upon the reciprocation of that love from another* kind of love associated with God and His creation and *philia*, the brotherly love that we tend to have towards one another.

I'm not so much interested in pursuing a discussion about brotherly love, that is something I think I can comprehend. It might be interesting to explore the part of the definition for *philia* that it is the love "between equals." After the Resurrection Jesus asks Peter three times, "Do you love me?"

The first time and the second time the Greek text reads "Do you *agape* me?" and the third time the Lord used *philia*, which could mean, "Peter, do you love me as an equal?" Peter agrees that he loves Jesus as an equal. That is a perfect example of how the Lord meets people where they are. The Bible doesn't record how Peter died, but it is commonly thought that he gave his life for his Lord and died hung inverted on a cross. In the end, Peter loved Jesus like Jesus loved him, in that he died for him. However, what I am interested in is that *self-sacrificing-no-matter-what kind of love that is not dependent upon the reciprocation of that love from another* love that God has for us and whether or not I am capable of loving like that.

I stated that love isn't an emotion or feeling. What is love? The best description of love is in the Bible:

> "Love is patient and is kind; love doesn't envy. Love doesn't brag, is not proud, doesn't behave itself inappropriately, doesn't seek its own way, is not provoked, takes no account of evil; doesn't rejoice in unrighteousness, but rejoices with the truth; bears all things, believes all things, hopes all things, endures all things." (1 Corinthians 13:4-7)

Notice in Paul's description that he never says anything about it being a feeling, emotion, or even something to do (often I hear that love is a verb). What he does do is define *agape* (love) as an attribute. An attribute: something attributed as belonging to a person, thing, group, etc.; a quality, character, characteristic, or property.[6]

Love is something you have, not something you feel or even something you do. It's something that is a part of you. It's an attribute like a sense of humor or sensitivity or kindness. Love is the basic blueprint for how you act and react to everyone and everything around you. Love is the characteristic that causes you to act a certain way. Love governs how you

6 Dictionary.com; noun, meaning #5

respond to your situation. You don't act that way because you love, but because love is a part of you. You can't help but act a certain way.

When the Bible speaks about God's love, it always talks about His demonstration of that love:

> "For God so loved the world, that he gave his one and only Son, that whoever believes in him should not perish, but have eternal life." (John 3:16)

> "But God commends his own love toward us, in that while we were yet sinners, Christ died for us." (Romans 5:8)

Which brings me back once again to the original question, am I capable of a *self-sacrificing-no-matter-what kind of love that is not dependent upon the reciprocation of that love from another?*

The answer to my question lies in the Scriptures. I read this about me in the Bible:

> "God said, "Let's make man in our image, after our likeness. Let them have dominion over the fish of the sea, and over the birds of the sky, and over the livestock, and over all the earth, and over every creeping thing that creeps on the earth." Genesis 1:26

> "I will give thanks to you, for I am fearfully and wonderfully made. Your works are wonderful. My soul knows that very well." (Psalms 139:14)

I am created in the image and likeness of God, and I am "fearfully and wonderfully made."

Then I come to another thing that Paul wrote:

> "and hope doesn't disappoint us, because God's love {*agape*} has been poured out into our hearts through the Holy Spirit who was given to us." (Romans 5:5)

Agape poured into my heart! From this, I know that I am capable of a *self-sacrificing-no-matter-what kind of love that is not dependent upon the reciprocation of that love from another.* Then I took another look at 1 John 4:19 in a translation that is from different (and earlier/older) manuscripts:

We love because He first loved us. (1 John 4:19 NASB)

We love because HE who created us made us with love and created us to love. Then He pours His love into us through the Holy Spirit. The problem must be on my part, either in realizing this is true or in the application of my life. Agape is in our hearts. It's there. The potential of a *self-sacrificing-no-matter-what kind of love that is not dependent upon the reciprocation of that love from another* is right here inside me. Not loving the way God does is wasting an incredible opportunity. It's no different than someone having the gift of writing and performing music or athletics but not exercising that ability.

Because of the difficulty above for my flesh to do what is good, I have come to realize is that any agape I demonstrate is the love of God manifesting through me.

"I have been crucified with Christ, and it is no longer I that live, but Christ lives in me. That life which I now live in the flesh, I live by faith in the Son of God, who loved me, and gave himself up for me." (Galatians 2:20)

Knowing that I can love that is a *self-sacrificing-no-matter-what kind of love that is not dependent upon the reciprocation of that love from another* is the first step on the path to demonstrating that agape. I must spend more time with God. I must endeavor to see others the way He sees us. As I walk with Jesus, I will eventually be able to answer that woman at church with "I love you too," and mean it.

Chapter Three
The Lord's Name In Vain

One of the differences between my youngest brother and I is that I profess to be a Christian, and my brother is a self-declared atheist. That's not as far apart as one would think. In a recent post on Facebook he stated that there are in fact over 3,500 known gods, and that if one claims to believe in only one, albeit, the "One, true god", then one is only slightly less atheistic than he is, since he doesn't believe in any of the 3,500+ gods and you believe in only one.

Whether intentional or not, he says some things that I find challenging from time to time. One weekend after I had moved to the Beaumont-Port Arthur Texas area for a job we were talking, and I mentioned that I was thinking about joining the worship team at a local church in Port Neches where I lived. I had spoken with the pastor, and he had informed me that he'd been praying for a guitar player. My brother thought that was funny and wondered how God had time to worry about such trivial things as a musician for a church in South East Texas when He has important things to do like pick football game winners and the Republican nominee. I took offense because I automatically assumed he was picking at Tim Tebow (I'm not sure if he was or not) when Tim Tebow has never claimed that God was influencing the outcome of the football game (it was Tebow's pastor). As far as I can tell, none of the people running for the Republican nomination have claimed that God has picked them (although two politically active pastors in Iowa did attempt to influence Michelle Bachmann or Rick Santorum to drop out of the race for the Republican nomination in Iowa in 2011 because they felt the 2 would split the evangelical vote). I wanted to retort, but Proverbs 20:3 states, "It is to one's honor to avoid strife, but every fool is quick to quarrel." I, of course, would be the fool if I were to engage some "defense."

The one thing that it did do makes me attempt to see the world through his worldview instead of mine. Paul writes:

> "For though I was free from all, I brought myself under bondage to all, that I might gain the more. To the Jews I became as a Jew, that I might gain Jews; to those who are under the law, as under the law, that I might gain those who are under the law; to those who are without law, as without law (not being without law toward God, but under law toward Christ), that I might win those who are without law. To the weak, I became as weak, that I might gain the weak. I have become all things to all men, that I may, by all means, save some. Now I do this for the sake of the Good News, that I may be a joint partaker of it." (1 Corinthians 9:19-23)

Paul was teaching that we need to approach people from their worldview and culture rather than our own without sacrificing our beliefs. This theme is evident in Rick Warren's book, "The Purpose Driven Church" and published it in 1995. The subtitle of the book is *growth without compromising your message and mission.* While I have often fallen short of "being all things to all people," I was making a serious attempt to view the world through his perspective. This task turned out to be more difficult than I had imagined. Here I am trying to relate to my brother, someone I share both parents with, grew up in the same house, and were taught the same values growing up, and yet, we have different worldviews. My disadvantage came due to our age difference. I am 11 years older than my brother. While he was a teenager, I had already gotten married and moved out. I became a Believer in my 30's so a lot of time had gone between when we lived in the same home and this discussion. Our religious beliefs color each of our worldviews, and I'll contend that everyone's worldview is colored by their religious beliefs, even if they claim not to have a religion. Neil Peart (drummer for the rock band Rush) was right when he wrote in the song, "Free Will":

> *You can choose a ready guide*
> *In some celestial voice*
> *If you choose not to decide*
> *You still have made a choice7*

A major part of my issue relating to people outside my perspective is I tend to surround myself with only "like-minded" people. Fellowshipping with other believers is a good thing. We are commanded to do so!

> "Let's consider how to provoke one another to love and good works, not forsaking our own assembling together, as the custom of some is, but exhorting one another; and so much the more, as you see the Day approaching." (Hebrews 10:24-25)

The danger of only associating with fellow believers is that doing this one cannot fathom how anyone can think differently than their usual group. Groupthink is one of the reasons many of us get "culture shock" when we go off to college. Suddenly one is thrust into a world where everyone doesn't think the same way as "we do back home." To even begin to appreciate my brother's perspective, I need to get out of my world and try to get into his.

For decades western missionaries set forth to spread the Gospel. They left western civilization to evangelize people with different cultures and worldviews and coerced them to conform to their idea of Christianity. For better or worse, that meant that people were forced to embrace western culture before they could accept our religion. This culture included

---

7 Neal Peart, *Freewill.* 1979 Mercury Records.

dressing a specific way to attend church services and reading the translation of the Bible preferred by the missionary. It worked to some degree, people did come to Christ, but it harkens back to the same problem Christianity had 2000 years ago! When non-Jews started coming to Christianity, there were plenty of Jews that wanted to require the new Gentile converts to adopt the Jewish traditions and culture, specifically physical circumcision and the dietary laws.

> "Some men came down from Judea and taught the brothers, "Unless you are circumcised after the custom of Moses, you can't be saved." Therefore, when Paul and Barnabas had no small discord and discussion with them, they appointed Paul and Barnabas, and some others of them, to go up to Jerusalem to the apostles and elders about this question. They, being sent on their way by the assembly, passed through both Phoenicia and Samaria, declaring the conversion of the Gentiles. They caused great joy to all the brothers. When they had come to Jerusalem, they were received by the assembly and the apostles and the elders, and they reported all things that God had done with them. But some of the sect of the Pharisees who believed rose up, saying, "It is necessary to circumcise them, and to command them to keep the law of Moses." The apostles and the elders were gathered together to see about this matter. When there had been much discussion, Peter rose up and said to them, "Brothers, you know that a good while ago God made a choice among you, that by my mouth the nations should hear the word of the Good News and believe. God, who knows the heart, testified about them, giving them the Holy Spirit, just like he did to us. He made no distinction between them and us, cleansing their hearts by faith. Now, therefore, why do you tempt God, that you should put a yoke on the neck of the disciples which neither our fathers nor we were able to bear?" (Acts 15:1-10)

In another passage, Paul calls out Peter for acting one way around the Gentiles and another way when he was with Jews. Peter couldn't act like a Gentile in Jewish company, but he expected the Gentiles to become Jews.

> "But when Peter came to Antioch, I {Paul} resisted him to his face, because he stood condemned. For before some people came from James, he ate with the Gentiles. But when they came, he drew back and separated himself, fearing those who were of the circumcision. And the rest of the Jews joined him in his hypocrisy; so that even Barnabas was carried away with their hypocrisy. But when I saw that they didn't walk uprightly according to the truth of the Good News, I said to Peter before them all, "If you, being a Jew, live as the Gentiles do, and not as the Jews do, why do you compel the Gentiles to live as the Jews do?" (Galatians 2:11-14)

When Western missionaries began to change their tactics to embrace local customs and cultures, Christianity started spreading like wildfire through Africa and South America. Currently, the majority of growth in the church is there. Now, missionaries from Africa are coming to the West to evangelize!

As I was pondering the situation, the most outrageous commercial came on the television. "Find God's match for you at ChristianMingle.com" ("You're Christian, you're single...(:23) sometimes we wait for God to make the next move when God is saying it's your time to act; the next move is yours..."

We have met the enemy, and he is us. –Walt Kelly

Is it any wonder that people outside the faith have such a low opinion of Christ when **we**, His followers, use His name to market products, use His name to influence politics, and use His name to declare favor for our social events? Is God picking winners and losers on the football field? Does He decide the point spread and then decide if either team covers it? What does it tell the non-believer to hear Wayne Hanson tell TMZ that "God is actively intervening on behalf of the Broncos because Tebow's faith is so strong."

> *Do you ever wonder just what God requires? You think He's just an errand boy to satisfy your wandering desires?*
> -Bob Dylan, *When You Gonna Wake Up?*

What does it tell the person outside the faith when pastors are telling us which candidate God has chosen? Is God truly a Republican or a Democrat? A Liberal or a Conservative? The Bible has to say about it:

> "Let every soul be in subjection to the higher authorities, for there is no authority except from God, and those who exist are ordained by God." (Romans 13:1)

Keep in mind that when Paul wrote this the ruler over him was Nero, a ruler that was using followers of "The Way" (i.e., Christians) for fuel to light his gardens at night. People write entire tomes explaining that God is a liberal or a conservative. The only thing we can be sure of is that for whatever His reason, God chose the current leaders over us.

C.S. Lewis warns about our mixing our religion with our politics in Letter VII in the Screwtape Letters:

> Let him begin by treating the Patriotism or the Pacifism as a part of his religion. Then let him, under the influence of partisan spirit, come to regard it as the most important part. Then quietly and gradually nurse him on to the stage at which the religion becomes merely part of the "cause"... Once you have made the World an end, and faith a means, you have almost won your man, and it makes very little difference what kind of worldly end he

is pursuing. Provided that meetings, pamphlets, policies, movements, causes, and crusades, matter more to him than prayers and sacraments and charity, he is ours — and the more "religious" (on those terms), the more securely ours. I could show you a pretty cageful down here...[8]

Many of our churches spend an extraordinary amount of time on politics and social justice. I'll talk about loving our neighbors in another chapter, but in the Kingdom of God, there are no liberals or conservatives, Democrats or Republicans. God's kingdom is just that, a *kingdom,* and He is the KING. One of Jesus' titles is "King of kings." Believers are kings (little "k") because they are *sons* of the King by adoption.

> "So then, brothers, we are debtors, not to the flesh, to live after the flesh. For if you live after the flesh, you must die; but if by the Spirit you put to death the deeds of the body, you will live. For as many as are led by the Spirit of God, these are children of God. For you didn't receive the spirit of bondage again to fear, but you received the Spirit of adoption, by whom we cry, "Abba! Father!" The Spirit himself testifies with our spirit that we are children of God; and if children, then heirs; heirs of God, and joint-heirs with Christ; if indeed we suffer with him, that we may also be glorified with him." (Romans 8:12-17)

We are our enemy because we continuously use the Lord's name in vain. How can we relate to another's viewpoint without compromising our own when we misrepresent our God?

You shall not use or repeat the name of the Lord your

---

8 C.S. Lewis, *The Screwtape Letters.*

God in vain [that is, lightly or frivolously, in false affirmations or profanely]; for the Lord will not hold him guiltless who takes His name in vain. Exodus 20:7 Amplified Bible

I use the Amplified Bible translation here to highlight the word "frivolously." When we attach the Lord's name to our products, social causes, politics, or anything else other than what He truly is, we are using the Lord's name in vain.

Chapter Four
Trading Truth For A Lie

Contemplating my death isn't something I like to do on a regular basis. In fact, I probably spend little to no time at all thinking about it at all. On the rare occasion when I do think about it, I assure myself that I'm not worried in the least about it because I am comforted by the fact that I know my destination. I believe in the promise of John 3:16, *For God so loved the world, that He gave his only Begotten Son, that whosoever shall believe in Him shall not perish, but have everlasting life*. I believe the blood of my Lord Jesus Christ paid for my salvation. Because of my faith in Him, I will spend eternity with Him.

Back when I worked for someone else, one of the companies I worked for had among its divisions a hospice. One time, the head of the hospice, Sherrie, was in my office chatting with another of my co-workers, Desiree, when the subject of death came up. Specifically, Desiree told Sherrie that she couldn't work in hospice care knowing all her patients were terminally ill and are going to die. Sherry looked at Desiree right in the eye and told her matter of fact, "We don't focus on the dying; we focus on living!" Being myself, I told Desirae that everyone she will ever meet dies eventually. Sherry then goes on to explain the more important aspects of her job like meeting someone that has lost weight and can't or won't eat, has no energy, etc., and then three weeks later seeing that same person eating and playing with their children or grandchildren and their pets. THAT is the focus.

Something else that hospice does is help people focus on their spirituality. It's unfortunate but true; many people don't seek out God until they realize their mortality. There's something to be said for realizing our mortality. The Bible tells us that "it is appointed for all men (i.e., all human beings) to die once, and then the judgment" (Hebrews 9:14). Suddenly, eternity is a priority. That statement touched me. I was telling my pastor, Jim, about it, and he said, "...that's God's mercy...most people don't have the luxury of knowing when and having a specific time to prepare. We have the promise of eternity but not for tomorrow."

The majority of the folk's hospice works with the transition to the next world peacefully. On this occasion, Sherry told us that she's only had a couple of patients that were atheists to the very end. I interjected at that moment, "I bet those two were afraid of dying!"

I was right.

She went on to describe one of the two. A self-declared atheist man that was not only without any spirituality, he was also hostile to and adamant about not having god or religion around him. His caregivers tending to him were required to either remove or cover up any jewelry or other markings that might indicate some religious significance (for example, a cross necklace). One nurse made the mistake of having her cross necklace come out of her shirt into plain view, and she was reported to the state for violating his religious freedom, or in this case, freedom from religion.

Sherrie continues, he was scared. There were people all around him, but he was alone. All he had was the current pain from his illness and the knowledge that he would soon be no more. He had nothing to comfort him. No hope for eternity. Nothing when air will no longer come into his lungs.

I have often contemplated why someone that doesn't believe in existence other than this material world fears death. If everything *ends*, why is there fear? I subscribe to the argument that I'd rather have my belief in Jesus and be wrong about it rather than to be the atheist that turns out wrong. I have hope and comfort. The other only has what he can perceive through the senses.

I can't help but think that even this man believed in God at the end. There's something about mortality that makes one look for something outside of their existence for comfort. However, he refused to acknowledge any "higher power" right up to his last breath. Paul writes about this in his letter to the Romans:

> "For the wrath of God is revealed from heaven against all ungodliness and unrighteousness of men, who suppress the truth in unrighteousness, because that which is known of God is revealed in them, for God revealed it to them. For the invisible things of him since the creation of the world are clearly seen, being perceived through the things that are made, even his everlasting power and divinity; that they may be without excuse. Because, knowing God, they didn't glorify him as God, neither gave thanks, but became vain in their reasoning, and their senseless heart was darkened. Professing themselves to be wise, they became fools and traded the glory of the incorruptible God for the likeness of an image of corruptible man, and of birds, and four-footed animals, and creeping things. Therefore God also gave them up in the lusts of their hearts to uncleanness, that their bodies should be dishonored among themselves; who exchanged the truth of God for a lie, and worshiped and served the creature rather than the Creator, who is blessed forever. Amen." (Romans 1:18-25)

The phrase that leaps off the page is *For they exchanged the truth of God for a lie.*

We can disagree on who God is (Jehovah, Allah, Krishna, Thor, etc.) or what His nature is, but I cannot understand how one can doubt whether He (or them, etc., just for the sake of keeping this civil!) exists at all. What makes life? There are currently 115 known elements in the universe. Everything we encounter, including each other, is made from combinations of these 115 elements. What is it that makes human beings alive when chemically we are not all that different from a shopping cart? Or to take it even further, what is different the instant after we die? Chemically our bodies are identical pre or postmortem.

At the risk of sounding like an ignorant religious nut, I'm going to say the answer is in the very beginning of the Bible. Genesis 1:3 reads, "Then God said, 'Let there be light' and BANG! there was light." If you ever look at a living cell under an electron microscope, you will see the most amazing thing. You see little sparks of light between the individual atoms. What is the source of this light?

Forgive me for quoting a new ager:

Imagine you're standing outside on the grass looking towards the sky. Hold your hands in the air and feel the heat of the sun, the movement of the wind brushing over your skin. As the wind touches your hand, it deposits molecules of every chemical needed to create life. As the sun warms your face, it radiates all the energy that generates life. We are nothing more than these chemicals, this energy, but with one tremendous difference: An invisible principle holds you together.

What is this invisible principle? Quite simply, God is this Invisible Principle. Because of this invisible principle, you were created out of the whirlwind of atoms that fly through the universe. Instead of being scattered inside a galactic dust cloud, your body has organized itself into thousands of precise operations. With every breath, you inhale hundreds of millions of gaseous molecules, and within a tenth of a second, the ones that sustain life, primarily oxygen and hydrogen, enter your cells to create enzymes and proteins.

How do they know to do this? They don't. The oxygen in your blood is no more alive than the oxygen in a diver's tank; the sugars in your brain are no more intelligent than those in a sugar cube. Yet the whirlwind turns into life somehow; the invisible principle causes this transformation.[9]

Although the principle cannot be seen nor weighted, it possesses certain qualities:

- It is intelligent - Omniscient
- It is conscious of itself
- It has power - Omnipotent
- It can organize things, creating complexity out of simplicity.

I chose to call this invisible principle God. While you and I can argue about the attributes of God, and we can argue about His (or her or it's) nature and about our relationship to our deity, if we are honest with each other, we cannot argue that there is or isn't a God. That anything is alive is such a calculated impossibility that there *must* be some designer. God operates in all life, and one cannot extract Him. There are just too many things that have to happen just right:

"...life cannot have had a random beginning...The trouble is that there are about two thousand enzymes, and the chance of obtaining them all in a random trial is only one part in 10 to the 40,000[th] power, an outrageously small probability that could not be faced even if the whole universe consisted of organic soup. If one is not prejudiced either by social beliefs or by a scientific training into the conviction that life originated on the Earth, this simple calculation wipes the idea entirely out of court...The enormous information content of even the simplest living systems...can not in our view be generated by what are often called "natural" processes...For life to have originated on the Earth, it would be necessary that quite explicit instruction should

9 One More Reality To Go (article) by Deepak Chopra

have been provided for its assembly...There is no way in which we can expect to avoid the need for information, no way in which we can simply get by with a bigger and better organic soup, as we ourselves hoped might be possible a year or two ago." Fred Hoyle and N. Chandra Wickramasinghe[10]

One of the great theological questions is, "How can one prove God exists?" Ironically, the Bible never sets out to prove God's existence. His existence is always assumed. I'm going to go out on a limb here and say that one doesn't have to prove God exists. God doesn't have to exist, God is. God doesn't have power; God is power. Goes doesn't have knowledge; God is knowledge, etc. GOD IS. The proof is in everything else that exists.

God is, man exists.

Sherry told us about the end of her patient. She was in the room when he passed on. As the moment arrived, his face and body began to contort in ways that a human body doesn't move. The contortions were like those described by people writing about exorcisms. As she was describing it, I could see demons grabbing him, pulling on his flesh, actually ripping the flesh from his body.

> "Knowing therefore the fear of the Lord, we persuade men, but we are revealed to God; and I hope that we are also revealed in your consciences." (2 Corinthians 5:11)

---

10 Evolution from Space [Aldine House, 33 Welbeck Street, London W1M 8LX: J.M. Dent & Sons, 1981), p. 148, 24,150,30,31).

Chapter Five
Acceptable Sins

On her radio show sometime before 2004, Dr. Laura Schlesinger regularly said that for her as an observant Orthodox Jew, homosexuality is an abomination according to Leviticus 18:22, and cannot be condoned under *any* circumstance. In December of 1998, on her radio show she is on record saying:

> *I'm sorry — hear it one more time, perfectly clearly: If you're gay or a lesbian, it's a biological error that inhibits you from normally relating to the opposite sex. The fact that you are intelligent, creative and valuable is all true. The error is in your inability to relate sexually intimately, in a loving way to a member of the opposite sex — it is a biological error.*

Thanks to her often-aired opinion that gay and lesbian individuals are a "mistake of nature," Dr. Laura became a lightning rod for those with pro-gay sympathies looking for someone to shake a finger. Around 2000 AD a letter written by Kent Ashcraft to Dr. Laura was sent to her asking her to clarify some other Bible verses as to his conduct. A brief excerpt:

> I have learned a great deal from your show, and try to share that knowledge with as many people as I can. When someone tries to defend the homosexual lifestyle, for example, I simply remind them that Leviticus 18:22 clearly states it to be an abomination. ... End of debate.
>
> I do need some advice from you, however, regarding some other elements of God's Law and how to follow them.

1) When I burn a bull on the altar as a sacrifice, I know it creates a pleasing odor for the Lord --Lev.1:9. The problem is my neighbors. They claim the odor is not pleasing to them. Should I smite them?
2) I would like to sell my daughter into slavery, as sanctioned in Exodus 21:7. In this day and age, what do you think would be a fair price for her?
3) Lev. 25:44 states that I may indeed possess slaves, both male, and female, from neighboring nations. A friend of mine claims that this applies to Mexicans, but not Canadians. Can you clarify? Why can't I own Canadians?

We know about the letter because after the author sent it to Dr. Laura, he sent it to a few of his friends thinking they'd find it amusing; they did. Many of them sent it to more of their friends thinking they'd find it amusing, and eventually, it went viral all over the Internet. It's amusing for sure, but the writer asks provocative questions about how he is supposed to handle various infractions of God's Law. Jews and Christians state that God is the same today, yesterday, and tomorrow. Prohibitions in the past should be prohibited now. The original intent of the letter was to point out the fallacy of using the Bible to condemn one thing when we as a culture, and society and specifically people that profess to read and believe the Bible now find acceptable. I find that the letter demonstrates how we as a culture respond to various things that were once totally unacceptable but are now okay. Why have some sins become *acceptable* to us?

Have you or anyone you've ever known gone to work on a Saturday?

> "'Six days shall work be done, but on the seventh day there shall be a holy day for you, a Sabbath of solemn rest to Yahweh: whoever does any work in it shall be put to death." (Exodus 35:2)

According to the Law of Moses, we should kill anyone doing any work on the Sabbath (Saturday). We laugh at that idea now, but at one time it was forbidden.

I'm personally responsible for eight people breaking the law written in Leviticus:

> "These you may eat of all that are in the waters: whatever has fins and scales in the waters, in the seas, and in the rivers, that you may eat. All that don't have fins and scales in the seas, and in the rivers, of all that move in the waters, and of all the living creatures that are in the waters, they are an abomination to you," (Leviticus 11:9-10)

Friday night we had friends over and served shrimp linguine. As far as I know, everyone in the room professes to be followers of Christ. We all claim to believe what the Bible says, yet not one of us thought *anything* of our eating shellfish other than it was delicious!

Often New Testament believers explain the end of the dietary laws with what God told the Apostle Peter in the vision of the sheet detailed in Acts 10.

> "A voice came to him, "Rise, Peter, kill and eat!" But Peter said, "Not so, Lord; for I have never eaten anything that is common or unclean." A voice came to him again the second time, "What God has cleansed, you must not call unclean." (Acts 10:13-15)

What God has cleansed, you must not call unclean is often taught to mean that the dietary restrictions have ended. However, the passage then goes on to tell Peter to go to the Gentiles and preach the gospel. Gentiles by the standards of the Jews were "unclean" and to avoid at all costs. It is the Gentiles that God is telling Peter not to call unclean. Peter himself interprets the vision this same way in Chapter 11 of Acts when he is in

Jerusalem telling the other apostles about the Gentiles that had received the Holy Spirit.

Last week in my Sunday school class' study of the *Letter to the Romans*, we got to the now controversial passage regarding homosexuality.

> "For this reason, God gave them up to vile passions. For their women changed the natural function into that which is against nature. Likewise also the men, leaving the natural function of the woman, burned in their lust toward one another, men doing what is inappropriate with men, and receiving in themselves the due penalty of their error. Even as they refused to have God in their knowledge, God gave them up to a reprobate mind, to do those things which are not fitting; being filled with all unrighteousness, sexual immorality, wickedness, covetousness, malice; full of envy, murder, strife, deceit, evil habits, secret slanderers, backbiters, hateful to God, insolent, arrogant, boastful, inventors of evil things, disobedient to parents, without understanding, covenant breakers, without natural affection, unforgiving, unmerciful; who, knowing the ordinance of God, that those who practice such things are worthy of death, not only do the same, but also approve of those who practice them." (Romans 1:26-32)

I approached these verses with fear and trepidation because I knew it is a hot topic among God's people. Sure enough, a passionate discussion ensued. *This* particular sin is not acceptable to some of us, a little more acceptable to others, and while not expressed out loud in the class, totally acceptable to others. Which, ironically, is the point that Paul (the author of the Letter to the Romans) was making with verses 1:26 to 32. That homosexuality is a sin we all agreed. Our disagreement was over how *acceptable* that sin is.

What about other sexual sins? Do we vary our acceptance of adultery? The Biblical definition of "adultery" is sex between individuals where at least one of the people engaging in it is married to someone else. How about lustful thoughts? Jesus said that if one even *looks* at another and thinks about sex that person has committed adultery in their heart.[11] What about self-gratification? Is self-gratification only a sin if the person engaging in it is married? Pretty much any sort of sex outside the marriage bed is considered sin by God. Everyone in the class agreed these too are sins, but how many of us excuse adultery because someone is unhappy in their marriage, or because the spouse is ill and unable to accommodate, or some other reason?

In her book *Sex, Lies and the Media*, Eva Marie Everson recounts the following story:

> "My friend Jack Samad with the National Coalition for the Protection of Children and Families shocked me with the story of his attendance at a religious convention. The manager of the hotel where he had been staying noticed the posters and other paraphernalia he had carried through the lobby early one morning and then back in again later that afternoon. He stopped Jack and asked him what he was doing with all that information on pornography. Jack told him he was part of the Christian conference being held in the city. The manager chuckled. "Get real," he said. Porn movies in our hotel are accessed at a higher rate during Christian conventions than at any other time."[12]

Other writers and journalists have investigated this claim and seemed to concur. How many of these same Christians that in secret view porn would openly condemn homosexuality? Why is this acceptable? Because others don't know about it?

---

11 Matthew 5:28
12 Eva Marie Everson and Jessica Everson. *Sex, Lies, and the Media.*
© 2005

The Bible has this to say about sexual sins:

> "Flee sexual immorality! "Every sin that a man does is outside the body," but he who commits sexual immorality sins against his own body." (1 Corinthians 6:18)

The one who commits sexual immorality sins against his own body. This statement makes sexual sin a category all to itself in the realm of sin. Paul then goes on with a list of other sins that are even viler for they show us our rebellious nature.

> "being filled with all unrighteousness, sexual immorality, wickedness, covetousness, malice; full of envy, murder, strife, deceit, evil habits, secret slanderers, backbiters, hateful to God, insolent, arrogant, boastful, inventors of evil things, disobedient to parents, without understanding, covenant breakers, without natural affection, unforgiving, unmerciful; who, knowing the ordinance of God, that those who practice such things are worthy of death, not only do the same but also approve of those who practice them." (Romans 1:29-32)

…knowing the ordinance of God, that those who practice such things are worthy of death, not only do the same but also approve of those who practice them.

What are some of our other "acceptable sins? At one time gambling was considered taboo. Today the lottery is promoted to help children. I've heard Christians claim that they play the lottery so that when they win, they can use the money for God's glory! How about swearing (i.e., cussing)? I've heard preachers utter profanities in private company. Alcohol? It wasn't all that long ago that drinking alcohol was so taboo they the United States passed a constitutional amendment forbidding it! Idolatry? Idolatry is anything you put more value into than God. That can include your cross necklace or your

Bible you keep in the back window of your car because you somehow believe it will protect your vehicle. How about greed? I've got another chapter called "The One With The Most Toys When He Dies Wins." Gluttony? How many obese people do we see in the church or on TV professing to be Christians? I once made this joke about my weight: I read in the Bible that my body is a temple of the Holy Spirit. I'm just building the biggest temple I can find!

There is an argument to be made that there are indeed *degrees of sin.* Jesus said:

> "Jesus answered, "You would have no power at all against me unless it were given to you from above. Therefore, he who delivered me to you has greater sin." (John 19:11)

One cannot have a "greater sin" unless there is a "lesser" one available. The parable of the moneylender also implies there are levels of sin.

> "A certain lender had two debtors. The one owed five hundred denarii, and the other fifty. When they couldn't pay, he forgave them both. Which of them, therefore, will love him most?" Simon answered, "He, I suppose, to whom he forgave the most." He said to him, "You have judged correctly." (Luke 7:41-43)

Before one begins to start romanticizing Dante's Inferno's version of punishment for sins, the Bible implicitly states that the penalty for sin is the same regardless of the severity of the offense. All sin separates us from God.

> "But your iniquities have separated you and your God, and your sins have hidden his face from you so that he will not hear." (Isaiah 59:2)

To summarize this passage, cultures, and societies tend to rationalize certain sins, but Scripture teaches that the penalty for sin is death.[13] God judges all sin.

It doesn't matter if one is predisposed to any particular sin. An excuse I hear often is "I can't help it; I was born this way." While this is an excuse, the statement is *true* for every one of us. The psalmist writes:

> "Indeed, I was born guilty, a sinner when my mother conceived me." (Psalms 51:5 NRSV)

Scripture teaches us that *all* have sinned and fallen short of the glory of God.[14] Ever since the incident in the Garden of Eden where both Adam and Eve disobeyed God has everyone that came after sinned.

> "Therefore, as sin entered into the world through one man {Adam} and death through sin; so death passed to all men because all sinned." (Romans 5:12) {emphasis mine}

What is the judgment for sin?

> "For the wages of sin is death, but the free gift of God is eternal life in Christ Jesus our Lord." (Romans 6:23)

Not even being aware that something is a sin doesn't excuse it either.

> "You shall do the same on the seventh day of the month for anyone who has sinned through error or ignorance; so you shall make atonement for the temple." (Ezekiel 45:20 NRSV)

---

13 Romans 6:23
14 Romans 3:23

We do not need to judge or condemn the lost and sinners. They do not require our condemnation. Discontinuing whatever sin we know we are doing doesn't take away the condemnation. I want to look specifically at John 3:18, but I like to put things in context:

> "For God so loved the world, that he gave his one and only Son, that whoever believes in him should not perish, but have eternal life. For God didn't send his Son into the world to judge the world, but that the world should be saved through him. He who believes in him is not judged. He who doesn't believe has been judged already because he has not believed in the name of the one and only Son of God. This is the judgment that the light has come into the world, and men loved the darkness rather than the light; for their works were evil. For everyone who does evil hates the light, and doesn't come to the light, lest his works would be exposed. But he who does the truth comes to the light, that his works may be revealed, that they have been done in God." (John 3:16-21)

He who believes is not condemned, but he who does not believe is condemned already because he has not believed in the name of the only begotten Son of God.

While counseling people that have been caught doing something wrong and are drawing the ire of their church family, I often comment, "The only difference between you and them is we now know what your sin is." How many of us stand in judgment of our brothers and sisters when we are practicing sin? Jesus addressed this too:

> "Don't judge, so that you won't be judged. For with whatever judgment you judge, you will be judged; and with whatever measure you measure, it will be measured to you. Why do you see the speck that is in your brother's eye, but don't consider the beam that is in your own eye?

Or how will you tell your brother, 'Let me remove the speck from your eye;' and behold, the beam is in your own eye? You hypocrite! First, remove the beam out of your own eye, and then you can see clearly to remove the speck out of your brother's eye." (Matthew 7:1-5)

By definition, the Christian has admitted to being guilty of sin, admitted they are powerless to do anything about it, and that they need a Savior. His name is Jesus.

Chapter Six
Good Bye To Religion

One of the things I had planned to do with the rest of my life was to go into full-time ministry. I've had others encourage me throughout my adult life (even before I was a Christian) and thought about it often. I've applied to seminary (ended up not going) and went through a two-year church planter training. I have concluded that I am a pitiful excuse for a pastor. In the first letter to Timothy, Paul writes that an overseer must be above reproach.

> "The overseer, therefore, must be without reproach, the husband of one wife, temperate, sensible, modest, hospitable, good at teaching;" (1 Timothy 3:2)

I look around at what people expect from their pastor and see that I'm woefully short. Occasionally I'll order a glass of wine or a mixed drink in public. From time to time an expletive will escape my mouth. Sometimes I can't help but look at an attractive woman. Other times I act like I only believe in 6 of the ten commandments. How can I possibly be a preacher when I either can't or won't act the way I perceive people think preachers are supposed to act?

I've mentioned this verse of Scripture in my writings before, but it bears repeating here.

> "For I don't know what I am doing. For I don't practice what I desire to do; but what I hate, that I do." (Romans 7:15)

People have interesting concepts about what a pastor does. In addition to being above reproach, a pastor is supposed to be available at every hour of every day to anyone for any reason whatsoever. Preachers are expected to spend every moment they are not being used by someone to pray, meditate, and study the Bible. Rather than study Scripture themselves or simply to pray, people expect their pastor to know the answer to every question and be able to point out the exact verse of Scripture that proves that answer. Pastors are expected to come running in the middle of the night after spending the whole day helping someone else. People come to their pastor right before church service and want to seek counsel. Pastors are expected to make the hospital runs, help move furniture, taxi people to and from the doctor or market, and that's before noon.

I fail.

People may demand more from their pastor than what people got from Jesus during His earthly ministry. Jesus was not available to the congregation non-stop.

> "Immediately Jesus made the disciples get into the boat, and to go ahead of him to the other side, while he sent the multitudes away." (Matthew 14:22)

One story that is taught often regards Peter healing a man:

> "Peter and John were going up into the temple at the hour of prayer, the ninth hour. A certain man who was lame from his mother's womb was being carried, whom they laid daily at the door of the temple which is called Beautiful, to ask gifts for the needy of those who entered into the temple. Seeing Peter and John about to go into the temple, he asked to receive gifts for the needy. Peter, fastening his eyes on him, with John, said, "Look at us." He listened to them, expecting to receive something from them. But Peter said, "I have no silver or gold, but what I have, that I give you. In the name of Jesus Christ

of Nazareth, get up and walk!" He took him by the right hand and raised him up. Immediately his feet and his ankle bones received strength. Leaping up, he stood and began to walk. He entered with them into the temple, walking, leaping, and praising God. All the people saw him walking and praising God. They recognized him that it was he who used to sit begging for gifts for the needy at the Beautiful Gate of the temple. They were filled with wonder and amazement at what had happened to him." (Acts 3:1-10)

A beautiful illustration of how we believers can do the works our Lord did. Hardly anyone notes when teaching from this Scripture that Peter and John probably saw that man begging at the Gate Beautiful *many times* before this day. That same beggar most likely solicited Peter multiple times before this day. Peter was not available 24 hours a day seven days a week!

I do spend time praying, meditating, and studying the Bible; however, I probably cannot answer every question about God that someone might have on demand. As my (both present and past) pastor(s) say, and I wholeheartedly agree, "the more I know about God, the more I know I don't know about God." I have too many questions myself to know the answers to all your questions.

Focus on the journey, not the destination. Joy is found not in finishing an activity but in doing it. ~Greg Anderson

As far as I can tell, entirely too many folks are content to depend on what someone tells them about God and piggyback a ride with their pastor and let their preacher do the traveling.

I've given up my plan to go into full-time ministry, but more importantly, I've had to say goodbye to religion. *Religion is the piggyback ride.* Religion tells folks what they believe. If you don't believe that, ask someone other than the resident Bible scholar at a church you don't attend what he/she believes. The odds are overwhelming they will send you to their pastor, a website, or a pamphlet. Have you ever had someone attempt to convert you and when you stump them with one of your questions or answers they volunteer to have you chat with their pastor? I have had that happen more times than I can count. If you're the preacher, you have invariably had the phone call, "Preacher, what do we believe about..."

Religion gives people a license to be lazy. It's a set of rules, regulations, and doctrines; a list of what to do, what not to do, what to believe, and what not to believe. Religion cannot possibly be of God, because God often reminds us to seek Him.

> "But from there you shall seek Yahweh your God, and you shall find him when you search after him with all your heart and with all your soul." (Deuteronomy 4:29)

> "Yahweh looked down from heaven on the children of men, to see if there were any who understood, who sought after God." (Psalms 14:2)

> "Without faith, it is impossible to be well pleasing to him, for he who comes to God must believe that he exists and that he is a rewarder of those who seek him." (Hebrews 11:6)

Religion tells me who to love and who to hate. Religion forces me to decide if I'm a Baptist or Methodist, a Catholic, Lutheran, Orthodox, Pentecostal, etc.... Once I decide what religion I am, religion defines how I must act and believe. Moreover, religion defines how I must judge you according to how you act or believe. Religion teaches me that if you don't believe exactly the way I do, you are part of a cult. Religion teaches me how to judge your relationship with God.

A pastor friend of mine is a janitor at another church for his day job. He was told recently about a conversation he had with someone at his work wholly convinced that anyone not a member of that specific denomination was not going to heaven. I think a lot of us are going to be surprised at who is and isn't there in heaven.

Denominations have to be the work of the Advisory. There is a story I heard about God and the devil walking one day. God tells the devil, "Hey, I've got this great idea, I call it religion…" To which the devil replies, "Great idea! Let me organize it!" Divide and conquer.

Listen to the words of Jesus as He prays for us:

> "I pray not that you would take them from the world, but that you would keep them from the evil one. They are not of the world even as I am not of the world. Sanctify them in your truth. Your word is truth. As you sent me into the world, even so, I have sent them into the world. For their sakes, I sanctify myself, that they themselves also may be sanctified in truth. Not for these only do I pray, but for those also who will believe in me through their word, that they may all be one; even as you, Father, are in me, and I in you, that they also may be one in us; that the world may believe that you sent me. The glory which you have given me, I have given to them; that they may be one, even as we are one; I in them, and you in me, that they may be perfected into one; that the world may know that you sent me, and loved them, even as you loved me." (John 17:15-23)

How can we be one when we spend so much time fighting each other? When the religious leaders of the day accused Jesus of being demonic, He said, "a house divided against itself cannot stand." (Mark 3:25) Religion is the great weapon of Satan to keep people from their God.

> I like your Christ; I do not like your Christians. Your Christians are so unlike your Christ. ~Mohandas Gandhi

One of the greatest compliments I get come from pre-believers who tell me I'm not like any other Christian they've ever met. The reason it's such a great compliment is that I don't make a point to tell people I'm a Christian, they figure it out themselves.

So I'm saying goodbye and so long to religion.

Jason Grey sings these lyrics:

> 'Cause all religion
> Ever made of me
> Was just a sinner
> With a stone tied to my feet[15]

What I've come to understand is God for some reason desires a *relationship* with His creation, with me, and with you. Why else would He *die* for us? The Bible says:

> "For all the fullness was pleased to dwell in him {Christ Jesus}; and through him to reconcile all things to himself, by him, whether things on the earth or things in the heavens, having made peace through the blood of his cross." (Colossians 1:19-20)

The key word in that passage is *reconciled;* "to restore friendly relations between individuals."

That God is interested in being reconciled must mean that somehow He and His Creation are estranged. The problem starts very early in the Bible. It began in Genesis 3 when both Adam and Eve willfully disobey God. Until that time God would walk in the cool of the evening and commune directly with Adam (and I assume Eve after her creation). Communion

---

15 *More Like Falling In Love*, Jason Grey, Jason Ingram, 2009
Centricity Music Publishing, So Essential Tunes Spirit Nashville Three Spirit Nashville Three

between God and humanity broke in a single act of disobedience.

Sin breaks our connection to God. Isaiah wrote that our inequities build barriers between God and us[16], yet, He *wants* to be in a relationship with us!

> "This is the message which we have heard from him and announce to you, that God is light, and in him is no darkness at all. If we say that we have fellowship with him and walk in the darkness, we lie and don't tell the truth. But if we walk in the light, as he is in the light, we have fellowship with one another, and the blood of Jesus Christ, his Son, cleanses us from all sin." (1 John 1:5-7)

"...we have *fellowship* with him..." Fellowship means "friendly association." That is a relationship! One cannot have a friendly association or reconcile with someone outside of the relationship. A king does not have "friendly associations" with peasants and commoners. A king has that type of relationship with family and friends and other royalty. God goes to extreme lengths to stay in fellowship with us. We cannot possibly be holy enough to be in a relationship with God, that was the whole lesson the Law and the Prophets (i.e., Old Testament) taught us. Paul refers to the Law as a tutor (schoolmaster in other translations):

> "But before faith came, we were kept in custody under the law, confined for the faith which should afterward be revealed. So that the law has become our tutor to bring us to Christ, that we might be justified by faith. But now that faith has come, we are no longer under a tutor. For you are all children of God, through faith in Christ Jesus." (Galatians 3:23-26)

---

16 Isaiah 59:2

Interesting is the word translated "schoolmaster" in that passage. It's from the Greek word, *paidagōgos*. While the word is correctly translated "schoolmaster", the word more precisely refers to the slave that was responsible for taking the master's children to school from age 6 or 7 till puberty. This is striking imagery of how the Law was primarily given for a certain purpose as an attendant to lead us to Jesus, who is the real teacher. The Law taught Mankind that we just can't live up to the expectations of a Holy God. Isaiah wrote

> But we are all like an unclean thing, And all our righteousnesses are as filthy rags; We all fade as a leaf, And our iniquities, like the wind, Have taken us away. (Isaiah 64:6 NKJV)

God desires reconciliation with all of humanity.[17] Time after time the Israelites turn away from God and time, and again He pursues them. On our own we could not be good enough to be in His presence, so He took on the extraordinary task of settling the debt of sin Himself.

So I am saying goodbye to religion. I am not, however, saying goodbye to my God. Jesus is the Word become flesh who willingly gave His life for mine so that I may continue my journey with God for eternity. I will enjoy the journey.

---

17 1 Timothy 2:4

Chapter Seven
Thursday Night

For the first time in my life that I can consciously remember, I was terrified. There was a very real possibility that I could lose both my wife and my unborn daughter at the same time and there was little to nothing I could do about it. Wednesday had started out normally enough, I got up, got dressed, and went to work. At work, I did whatever it is I do there. Sometime around 10:30 AM Rachel sent me a text stating she was going to take a bath. I went about my day normally. The ringer on my phone was off and set to vibrate because I get a lot of text messages and it disrupts my workplace so I keep it silent and check it when I can. About noon I got ready to go to lunch and noticed that I had missed several calls from Rachel and that she had left a voicemail. That in of itself was unusual, so I immediately called her back. "What's up?"

"Come …. Home…. Pain…." was all she could get out. I had no idea what she was talking about in the message. How did she go from taking a bath to being incoherent? I tried talking to her on the phone, but she couldn't communicate. I immediately headed home. When I got home, I found her on the floor curled up in a ball moaning and screaming.

While Rachel and I were dating and engaged to be married, I brought up the subject of children. I had two adult children and wasn't necessarily interested in having more; however, Rachel had no children of her own, so I felt I needed to approach the subject before our wedding. "Oh Baby! I don't need any kids! I need you!" In my mind, that was the end of it, and I was content. However, I was also doing my family's genealogy and suddenly carrying on my name was important to me. I have two brothers and a sister. My oldest younger brother has two daughters of his own so they won't carry on our name; my youngest brother doesn't date as far as I can tell and I'm convinced he's a bachelor for life, and my sister's children will bear her husband's last name. My father has one brother and two sisters. His brother only had one daughter. The entire Powell family line depends on my first born! No pressure son!

One Saturday my new bride and I were visiting my mom and my older younger brother and his family. My brother and I were in one room watching the Dallas Cowboys game when I overhear my new wife telling my mother: "Danny wants to have another son to carry on the Powell name..." I, of course, have to jump up and run to the dining room where this discussion is taking place.

"I never said anything about having more kids. I specifically said I didn't want to have any more!"

Mom was having none of my protests. "She doesn't have any kids, you give that girl a baby!" my mother said. The fix was in. She dun got mama involved.

For whatever reason, getting pregnant was no small feat. For three years we tried and tried and month after month Rachel would cry when her time of the month came around. Our faith was tested continuously during this time because of the fertility issue. I comforted my wife with one of God's promises:

> "He gives the barren woman a home, making her the joyous mother of children. Praise the LORD!" (Psalms 113:9 NRSV)

So now here is my wife, 24 weeks pregnant, with incredible pain in her abdomen. How can the current situation be good? It took three years of conscious attempts to get pregnant. Up till this very moment (and we had seen the obstetrician that Monday), the pregnancy was textbook and her OB was making fun of her being the healthiest pregnant woman on the planet. At this moment both she and I are thinking that we are about to lose our baby.

I loaded her in the car and headed to the closest emergency room, Baptist Hospital in Beaumont, Texas. Since she's pregnant, emergency sends her straight up to labor and delivery. Alas, there was no room in the inn, so they had us wait a couple of hours in the waiting room till someone would see us. I don't fault the labor and delivery people, all they knew was there is a pregnant woman with abdominal pains. They assumed she was there to give birth. While sitting in the labor room, Rachel between moans told me that she could feel Olivia kicking and that she's okay.

When they finally got her into triage, the nurse was surprised to find out we were not expecting to deliver a baby today. We are only 24 weeks pregnant. The nurse asked about symptoms, and none of them seemed to indicate that Rachel was in labor. The nurse hooked up machines to monitor both mother and child. Baby's heartbeat was nice and healthy. The first theory was dehydration. That seemed plausible to me. Now, I'm not sure why. I suppose I just wanted the easiest and quickest diagnosis.

Rachel's obstetrician happened to be out on vacation, so the on-call OB had to make some diagnosis. In the best "Dr. House" fashion, without ever seeing the patient, he theorizes the problem might be appendicitis and orders an ultrasound of the abdomen. I Googled the symptoms and the symptoms matched. I was impressed with the OB. About half an hour later someone shows up with an ultrasound machine.

On the way to the hospital, I text messaged Rachel's mother, our pastor, and my sister who I knew would contact everyone else in the family with updates.

By the time the ultrasound tech arrived, it was almost 4 'o clock in the afternoon. Rachel had been in a ten-scale pain ten since about 10:30 that morning. No pain meds without a prescription, and so far we hadn't seen a doctor. Her mother arrived and shortly after that our pastor, David, joined us. David comforted me in the hall while I updated him on the situation, then he came in and along with Rachel's mom we have the most incredible intercessory prayer meeting I can ever remember.

The tech performs the ultrasound.

In our haste to get to the hospital, I neglected to pick up anything that might remotely suggest we might be in the hospital more than a few uncomfortable hours. Diane, Rachel's mom, sent me with her debit card to pick up supplies. When I get back, the nurses are finally giving her Demerol. 10:30 to sometime after 6:00 in constant incredible pain. The diagnosis has come back; her gallbladder is "full of stones."

Later that night a surgeon comes to see Rachel. He tells us that the only real solution is to remove the gallbladder, but that isn't preferred while a woman is pregnant. What they are going to attempt is to get the inflammation and swelling down on her gallbladder, and then send us home after about three days with a strict low-fat diet to get through the pregnancy and then have the surgery sometime after Olivia is born.

Late that evening I finally go home to take care of Daisy, my box terrier. I'm texting back and forth with Rachel, and I manage to sleep through the night.

Thursday morning comes. The issue now is that they are giving Rachel Demerol every 3 hours, but the relief from the drug only lasts about 20 minutes. The labor and delivery nurses are amazed that with a full dosage of Demerol she is still in such incredible pain. The pain continues through the night and the next day. We are somewhat relieved to know our unborn daughter is healthy. Thursday night the surgeon comes in to see Rachel. He looks at her and says, "You don't look any better now than when you first came in. You should be getting better, not worse. Even on Demerol, I can tell you are in a lot of pain." He tells us that he'll order another ultrasound in the morning and that depending on what he sees, we'll look at options at that point. Thirty minutes after he leaves an ultrasound tech arrives to do the procedure.

"Oh, Dr. Humble told us you were going to do that in the morning," I told her. She replied that the order he gave said STAT, meaning, as soon as possible. "Oh, okay, well, go ahead then." The ultrasound technician does the procedure, and after she leaves, I go home to take care of my dog again. Forty-five minutes after I leave Rachel texts me that she couldn't eat or drink anything (including ice chips) after midnight. That's odd, I thought, I thought he was going to review the ultrasound and then we were going to discuss options?

Rachel texts me that the nurses have told her that the doctor's order pretty much means they are doing surgery in the morning. I begin to worry. At 24 weeks, Olivia is nearly fully developed except for her young lungs. There is a risk of nicking the uterus during the surgery. If the surgeon cuts the uterus, they have to deliver the child via c-section. The odds are not good for Olivia if they have to take her out of the womb. This danger is why they don't like to do this surgery while a woman is pregnant. I don't want Rachel in pain, but I know that Rachel is the toughest woman on the planet and she'd rather tough this out than lose her baby.

At home, I begin pondering the entire situation. We went from thinking we were losing our baby on Wednesday afternoon to thinking we were going to be in the hospital for three days and go home to probable surgery first thing in the morning, again with the possibility that we were going to lose our baby. I prayed. Then I meditated. It was decision time. Do I believe all this stuff I profess or do I lose faith if we do indeed lose our baby? I had to ponder what my reaction to my friends and family, many of whom do not share my beliefs, will be if I lose my child. Can I still claim God is good and loving and all that if He allows my baby to die?

"Though he slays me, yet will I trust in him: but I will maintain mine own ways before him." (Job 13:15, KJV)

That verse spoke to me. The bottom line is where else is there I could go? What hope is there if I forsake the LORD? I grieve for atheists because where do they get comfort? Where do they get hope? From the inner self? What happens when we fail? From the "goodness" of humanity? My experience is that people will let you down.

> "And said, Naked came I out of my mother's womb, and naked shall I return thither: the LORD gave, and the LORD hath taken away; blessed be the name of the LORD." (Job 1:21 KJV)

Whether I like it or not, whether I think it's fair or not, the fact of the matter is that bad things do happen to good people. Also, every believer I've ever met or ever known either has died or will die. Some of natural causes, some of the more tragic variety.

> "Inasmuch as it is appointed for men to die once, and after this, judgment," (Hebrews 9:27)

Outside of the Bible, there is no record of any human being not dying! (In the Bible there are two such individuals, Enoch and Elijah).

In my prayer and meditation time, I make a conscious decision. Regardless of how this all turns out, I will remain strong in my faith. I posted this on Facebook:

> Immediately the father of the child cried out and said, "I believe; help my unbelief!" (Mark 9:24 ESV)

The prognosis is surgery in the immediate future for Rachel & Olivia. I prayed tonight on the way to the house to take care of Daisy, and this was my prayer. I finally decided that regardless of how this turns out, I either believe all this stuff I profess or I don't, and I am going to choose to trust God with all my being. God's work in mine & Rachel's life has thus far been beyond measure. I trust everything will work out in a way that I want (i.e., Rachel & Olivia are okay)

In the morning I'm there bright and early to make sure I don't miss the surgeon's visit. He walks in about 7:30 and informs us, "We're taking out your gallbladder this morning." Nothing about it being an option or one of many options, just matter-of-fact. I inquire about the baby. He tells me, "In cases like these, we take the life of the mother over the life of the baby. If we don't do this surgery now and the gallbladder ruptures, all the toxins, and stones in there will go into the small intestine, and your wife will most likely die. If she dies, the baby dies." Whether he said those exact words or if that's just how I remember them I'm not sure, but he did make it abundantly clear that we were taking out the gallbladder today. Dr. Humble, the surgeon on call at the hospital, just happened to be a specialist in laparoscopic surgery. Laparoscopic procedures are very minimally invasive and much safer for our baby rather than the more traditional "open flap" method. The danger with the open flap is rupturing the uterus, and if that happens, the baby has to come out via a C-section. They scheduled her for 10:30 and the procedure should take about an hour and a half.

Sometime around 10:00 AM, my pastor David showed up to pray with us. David waited with me during the entire surgery. We waited till 1:30. We expected to wait one and a half hours, but instead, we waited over three.

Finally, Dr. Humble comes out to the waiting room. It is customary for the surgeon to come out and talk to the family member waiting to discuss the surgery. Rachel went in for a 90-minute surgery that may or may not end the life of our daughter. That I don't see him for more than twice the amount of time we expected can't be good, can it? 2 hours in I see the anesthesiologist that took Rachel to surgery walking through the hospital hallway on her way to lunch. "Hey! Shouldn't you be taking care of my wife?" Finally, after I'd been waiting over three and a half hours, I see Dr. Humble come into the waiting room. I'm a bit anxious to hear what he has to say. The good news is his face doesn't indicate any bad news is about to come. Matter of fact, he seems *elated*. " "Those were the biggest gallstones I've ever seen! I might have to write an article about these," he said as he tossed two photographs on the table before me. "She had two stones almost 2.5 centimeters in diameter. Seven total. These didn't form in the last year. These stones have been forming for years." He's just going on and on about how big her gallstones are. I was getting frustrated because the last time we spoke (7:30 that morning) he was telling me I might not have a daughter...

I interjected, "HOW IS OLIVIA?"

Pause. I could tell his brain was switching gears. "Oh, she's just fine..." Then he went back to waxing poetic about the stones and what he had to do to get them out safely for Rachel and Olivia. In retrospect, I can appreciate his geekiness regarding the surgery. It was something *different* from his normal day to day routine. He had to figure out in mid-stream of the original surgery plan how to proceed. It turned out he ended up doing a modified open-flap surgery because the gallbladder was simply too large to come out through traditional laparoscopic methods. He started out laparoscopic and then modified the technique in that he only cut her open just enough to work and avoid the possibility of cutting issues with the uterus.

It's amazing how one can see the hand of God after an event like this. While in the depths of our problems, we often feel that God has overlooked us or is there to punish us outright. However, consider the story of Jonah in the belly of a fish for three days. Jonah was tossed from the ship he was on into the sea to drown. He says:

> You hurled me into the depths, into the very heart of the seas, and your currents swirled about me; all your waves and breakers swept over me. The engulfing waters threatened me; the deep surrounded me; seaweed was wrapped around my head. To the roots of the mountains, I sank down; the earth beneath barred me in forever. (Jonah 2:3, 5-6 NIV)

That is his prayer from *inside* the fish. While in that fish I'm sure he thought that God was punishing him or at the very least He had abandoned him, but as I discovered recently, the exact opposite was true. What looked like the depths of despair to Jonah turns out to be his salvation.

Instead of allowing Jonah to perish in the sea, The Lord provides a sanctuary in the belly of a fish. Left to his own devices, Jonah surely would have died in the sea either through consumption by a less generous life form (shark anyone?), or he would have simply drowned. Not only did the Lord provide a safe place for Jonah, but He also provided him with all the sushi Jonah could eat!

We found out later that Dr. Humble is *the* top surgeon in the Golden Triangle (Beaumont-Orange-Port Arthur Texas) area and that people from all over the world come to him for surgery. He just "happened" to be the surgeon on call when we came to the hospital.

We thought we moved to the Golden Triangle to pursue a job opportunity. However, we were only there for a year. Just long enough for Rachel to finally get pregnant (an answer to an earnest prayer after three years) and also to have her gallbladder that had been making stones for years (we thought she was lactose intolerant; the symptoms are very similar). Coincidence? We don't believe that. The word "coincidence" isn't even in the Scripture. Rachel and I both are convinced that the LORD guided us to Beaumont for the very purpose of having our child and having the best surgeon around deal with the stones. We moved back to Nacogdoches two weeks after Olivia was born.

Fortunately, I did not have to decide how I'm going to deal with a loss at that time. Both Rachel and Olivia recovered from the surgery just fine.

Chapter Eight
Learning to Pray

I often wonder why we find it so hard to pray. Not all of us, mind you, but the vast majority of us. I've had countless people ask me to pray for them. I don't mind praying for others; I consider it an honor, but while probing deeper, I find that people want me to do it because they think that I'm somehow more connected to God than they could be or that I know some great secret prayer formula.

My friend Michelle once asked me to pray for her uncle. She started out by telling me she doesn't "believe in all that stuff, but I know you do." I told her that she could ask God to heal her uncle just as good as I could, but she wasn't buying it. So I told her that what I'd be willing to do it, but rather than pray for her uncle later in secret, I'd do it right there and then with her.

"Oh no! Just do it when you pray!" she said.

"I need you to pray with me because we both have to agree on the outcome."

She laughed at me.

Long story short, a week later we're chatting, and she said, "I don't know what *you* did, but my uncle is doing GREAT! The doctors can't understand it."

I asked, "Do you believe now?" Jesus once said:

> "Jesus, therefore, said to him, "Unless you see signs and wonders, you will in no way believe." (John 4:48)

So why don't we believe?

One Sunday night while we were still dating, my (now) wife Rachel needed to pray for a friend of hers. She told me she didn't know what to do. I told her, 'there's nothing you can do. You can't fix her problem. All you can do is pray to Jesus to help her. He's the only one that can fix us anyway."

Monday morning, she text messaged me, "Teach me to pray."

The disciples once asked Jesus, "Lord, show us how to pray." And He did. I didn't think I could improve on what the Lord taught, so I directed her to read what Jesus said:

> "In this manner, therefore, pray: Our Father in heaven, Hallowed be Your name. Your kingdom come. Your will be done On earth as it is in heaven. Give us this day our daily bread. And forgive us our debts, As we forgive our debtors. And do not lead us into temptation, But deliver us from the evil one. For Yours is the kingdom and the power and the glory forever. Amen." (Matthew 6:9-13 NKJV)

I told her this is the model prayer. Just reciting this prayer defeats its intent; however, there isn't anything in the world wrong with reciting it. The prayer was good enough for Jesus; it's good enough for us. The purpose of the model prayer is to teach us how to pray, not an incantation to say.

Then I broke it down for her, "Our Father in heaven, Hallowed be Your name." This line is the opening. First, you address God. What I told her is it wasn't mandatory to be so formal when addressing God. She could say, "God," "Father," "Jesus," "Daddy," etc....

> "And because you are children, God sent out the Spirit of his Son into your hearts, crying, "Abba, Father!" (Galatians 4:6)

The word *Abba* is an Aramaic word that would most closely translate to "Daddy." It was a common term that young children would use to address their fathers. It signifies the close, intimate relationship of a father to his child, as well as the childlike trust that a young child puts in his "daddy."

Rachel said to me, "I can't call Him, 'Daddy'!" Why not? The Apostle teaches that we can and should. The relationship between God and the believer is often described in terms of sons and daughters. The point, of course, is that we may talk to God just like we speak to each other, addressing the person you are speaking too. When she talks to me, she doesn't usually say, "Mr. Powell", or "Husband" or "Danny Powell", she addresses me by her nickname for me, "Babylove" (which I don't care for *at all* but I love her, and I know who she's addressing!) If I want to be formal, I guess I could say, "Mrs. Powell" or "WIFE!" Often, I address her by my pet name for her, "Sunshyne."

The second part of that is, "hallowed be Your name." Hallowed means "magnificent," "blessed," "exalted," "awesome," you get the idea.

Sunshyne said, "So I could just start with, 'Jesus, You Rock!'"

I cried.

She got it. It can be that simple. Usually, I prefer to spend a bit more of my prayer time telling God how great He is. I know he knows, but I think He likes to hear me say it. I know my wife knows I love her, but she likes me to tell her from time to time. I know my daughters and my son know I love them too, but they like to hear it every now and again too.

The first lines of our prayer could be, "Jesus, You rock! I love you."

So often we try to make it difficult to talk to our God. But the word "Abba" is quite literally "daddy" or "papa." That would seem to indicate some intimate relationship. For all my plain talk about plain talk, I usually address God as Lord or Father, or Jesus.

The next part of the model prayer is, "Your kingdom come; Your will be done, on earth as it is in heaven." This is a surrendering verse. Not what I want, Lord, but what You want.

Even Jesus at the Mount of Olives before the crucifixion, He prayed, "Your will, not mine" (Luke 22:42). Whatever Your will is, Lord, that I want too. There's a freedom in surrender that I can't put into words just yet. I know that the more I surrender to the LORD, the more freedom I have. Maybe it's a trust thing; I don't know. I believe that God wants what is best for me always. I believe He wants to have an intimate relationship with me. It is His will. He died for me. I remember a few years ago when I used to recite the "Lord's Prayer" over and repeatedly as part of a meditation exercise. Gradually, the prayer became, "Your will be done on earth, in me, as it is in heaven."

"Give us this day our daily bread…" this is where we tell God what we want, need, and desire. Paul continued this teaching with:

> "In nothing be anxious, but in everything, by prayer and petition with thanksgiving, let your requests be made known to God." (Philippians 4:6)

There isn't anything I can't ask. This place in the prayer is also a good place to pray for others. Tell God what you want Him to do for others. Ask for their healing or their employment; or their salvation or their restoration. You may ask whatever you want to ask Him.

"Forgive us our debts as we forgive our debtors." This is a prayer for repentance. Fancy word meaning that we know we mess up and have to turn away from those things we know are wrong and turn back to God. Forgiving others teaches us what God does for us. It also teaches us what love (agape) is. Hard not to repent when you are asking for forgiveness and at the same time forgiving others.

"Lead us not to temptation but deliver us from the evil one." The Bible teaches us that the Lord tempts no man:

"Let no man say when he is tempted, "I am tempted by God," for God can't be tempted by evil, and he himself tempts no one." (James 1:13)

This line in the prayer is a prayer for protection. We've told God what we think about Him, we've asked for His will be done, and we've told Him what we want, need, and desire, we've asked for forgiveness, and now we ask Him to protect us.

"A Psalm by David. Yahweh is my shepherd: I shall lack nothing. He makes me lie down in green pastures. He leads me beside still waters. He restores my soul. He guides me in the paths of righteousness for his name's sake. Even though I walk through the valley of the shadow of death, I will fear no evil, for you are with me. Your rod and your staff, they comfort me. You prepare a table before me in the presence of my enemies. You anoint my head with oil. My cup runs over. Surely goodness and loving-kindness shall follow me all the days of my life, and I will dwell in Yahweh's house forever." (Psalms 23:1-6)

"For Yours is the kingdom and the power and the glory forever, Amen." A great way to end your prayer. It's all God's anyway, including us:

"Or don't you know that your body is a temple of the Holy Spirit who is in you, whom you have from God? You are not your own, for you were bought with a price. Therefore glorify God in your body and in your spirit, which are God's." (1 Corinthians 6:19-20)

For people learning to pray, the "Lord's Prayer" is an awesome example. (I put "Lord's Prayer" in quotes because this is the "model prayer," I think Jesus' prayer in John 17 is the actual Lord's Prayer.) I can't find any real reason not to recite it for a while. As you are training yourself to pray, say each line, pause, meditate on it, and then say anything you'd like to add, then go on to the next line.

Here's an example of using the model. See if you can spot all the parts.

Jesus, you rock. You do. I can't believe how awesome you are. Every time I think about your sacrifice for me I cry. Really. What's up with that? Anyway, I'm glad you did. You've changed my life so much in such a short time. I want to ask you to keep working on me. I know I'm not perfect yet, but I keep reading in your book that you'll make me perfect if I just let you. I want that, Lord. Really. Today has been a great day. Thanks. I appreciate that. I'm a little concerned about being behind in my school work and getting those cookbooks out on time at work. A little direction there would be great! Also, I need to pray for Kirk; his daughter told me today that he's home with pneumonia. I know you can handle that one, so get to it! I know you're perfecting me and all, but today I think I slipped up more than usual. I could use some help with that. I thought after I got saved I wouldn't have those thoughts anymore, but here I am dealing with them daily. Sorry about that. And while we're at it, why am I so mad at my boss? I guess I should realize that since he is the boss what he thinks is important is important. So, Lord, I want to ask that you keep me from having those thoughts and keep me focused on You. You are the Lord. Period. God, I pray these things in Jesus' name. Amen.

Chapter Nine
How Much Are You Worth?

There was a young man that was feeling worthless. People in his life were telling him he was worthless and he seemed to fail at everything he did. Distraught and hopeless, he went up a mountain seeking the advice of the wise old man. As the young man approached the top of the mountain, he was disappointed once more to discover the wise old man was getting up to go down from the mountain.

"Old wise man! I need your advice. I am distraught and melancholy because everyone says I am worthless."

The wise old man was in a hurry and said to him, "You'll have to come back. I'm in a big hurry and need to go somewhere."

Feeling rejected yet again, the young man cried out, "Won't anyone help me?"

The wise old man stopped and turned towards the young man. "I need to go, but if you do this small thing for me, I'll help you when I get back." Then he took off the ring from his pinky finger, and he handed it to the young man. "I need you to take this into town and sell it for me. Go to as many people as you need, but don't take any less than one gold coin for it."

The young man appeared resigned. "Sigh, okay, I'll do it. I'll come back tomorrow after selling the ring."

The young man took the ring to the marketplace and offered it for sale to everyone he came into contact. No one would offer him a gold coin. Some offered a bronze coin, others a silver coin, but no one offered the value of a gold coin.

The next day the young man made the trek up the mountain to meet the wise old man again. When he got there, he told the wise man, "Your ring isn't worth one gold coin. I showed it to everyone, and the most anyone would offer is one silver coin." Then he handed the ring back to the wise man. The wise old man took the ring and held it in his hand for just a moment before handing it back to the young man. "Do me one more favor. Take the ring to the jeweler and ask what he will give you for it."

Reluctantly, the young man took the ring again. He thought to himself, what a waste of time! I need actual help, and this guy has me trying to sell his worthless ring!

He took the ring to a jeweler. Upon seeing the ring, the jeweler's eyes lit up. He examined the ring with bright lights and a loupe. He weighed the ring; he took measurements. When he finished, he came back to the boy. "I have to have this ring, the craftsmanship of this ring is beyond astonishing. Only the purest select gold and platinum was used. All it needed was a little polishing to see it. And the jewels! I'm sure I've never seen stones of this quality before. There isn't another like it in all the world. All I can give you today is five gold coins, but if the old man can wait, I'll give him seven gold coins for it."

The young man couldn't believe what he just heard and had the jeweler repeat it. Afterward, he ran up the mountain to tell the wise old man the news. "YOUR RING IS WORTH 7 GOLD COINS!"

The wise man took the ring and put it back on his finger. "Two days ago you thought the ring was worthless based on the opinions of everyone you came into contact. Today, after taking it to an expert, you have discovered it's true worth. Why are you letting everyone's opinion dictate how much you are worth? You need to talk to an expert."

Psychologists tell us that there are three ways we look at ourselves. The first is how we perceive ourselves. It's what we think about ourselves, how we see ourselves. The second is what other people think about us, and the third one is how we think other people think about us. Not one of the three usually has anything to do with the other. The way other people perceive us is almost always very different than how we view ourselves and the way we think those people view us in most cases isn't even close to how they do.

Isn't it interesting how we perceive what people are worth? If I ask you what Bill Gates is worth, most people would say millions. If I ask you how much an unemployed, homeless drug addict alcoholic man sleeping on a park bench is worth most of us would think, "not much" or worse, "nothing." We tend to think of worth in dollars and cents. This is how we estimate the worth of people outside our inner circle of family and friends. What about the worth of people inside our circle of families and friends?

What is anything worth? The word, "worth" generally gets people thinking regarding dollars and cents but worth is so much more. Worth is determined by what someone is willing to give up for something else. Worth is the value of something not only in monetary terms, but in time; "This project took a lot of my free time to accomplish, but it was worth it." Integrity; "whatever she tells you, you can take that to the bank, she is a woman of worth." When we think about our friends and families, we tend to think in different terms other than dollars and sense. Our children are precious, priceless. Parents often will sacrifice their comfort, fortune, and health to give their children everything possible. For some of us, our spouses are priceless. For others, our spouse is worthless. Some of us have similar feelings towards someone in our family or extended family. In our families, we tend to value people for how they treat us and what they contribute to the family.

And then there is how we value ourselves. How much are any of us worth? There have been countless lessons about pride and thinking more of ourselves than we really should. Sermon after sermon about how great God is and how low we are. Miserable, worthless sinners. Wretched man that I am. But how much are any of us worth? Are we "worthless sinners," are we "worms"? Never mind what people tell us about ourselves, what do we tell ourselves?

Do we tell ourselves that we are too fat, too thin, too tall, too short? Do we tell ourselves that our hair is the wrong color or style, or that we don't have enough hair? Do we tell ourselves that we don't deserve to feel good about ourselves? Do we tell ourselves that we're not smart enough? Do we tell ourselves that it's wrong that other people have it better or worse than we do?

We do all kinds of things to try to get people to value us. We pick our wardrobe to gain people's affection; we work on our hair and our bodies to gain people's attention. We constantly strive to be worth something to other people. The question is how much do any of us think we are worth if we are constantly trying to prove our worth to other people?

When I talk to people and try to tell them about the great love of Christ, I get all kinds of reactions. Most of them have something to do with how they don't deserve it. "I'm not worth His time." "I'm not good enough," "Me and God got an understanding, I don't mess with Him, He doesn't mess with me." I try to tell them that God accepts them just as they are. "But Danny, you don't KNOW what I've done! God can't possibly want me!"

So how much are any of us worth? Should we go out into the marketplace and ask this question? To the world, we are nothing other than a commodity. Something to be used and discarded. People only give you worth by what they think they can get from you. Once obtained from you, you can be discarded! (Cynical, anyone?) If someone thinks you're worth a gold coin, would they offer only a silver one to obtain you? Harsh, yes, but when one considers what all we do to improve our value and then looks at all people do to destroy that same worth, it appears few of us have any clue. It would seem the ultimate authority on that would be God, the One who created us. The human brain is one of the most complex "machines" in the universe yet the world would have us believe something this complex came about through random chance and not by design. We truly have exchanged truth for a lie.

At this moment it seems as though science will never be able to raise the curtain on the mystery of creation. For the scientist who has lived by his faith in the power of reason, the story ends like a bad dream. He has scaled the mountains of ignorance; he is about to conquer the highest peak; as he pulls himself over the final rock, he is greeted by a band of theologians who have been sitting there for centuries. ~Robert Jastrow[18]

I believe that our God is all-knowing, all-powerful, everywhere at all times. God knows our hearts, God knows our minds, He is God, and we are what we are. What we know about the nature of God is written in our Scriptures. Regardless of the method (entire tomes have

been dedicated to how we were created), I believe God created everything that is seen and unseen. He is the Creator and ultimate authority on our value. He is the "expert." Let us look at what God has to say about our worth.

"For you formed my inmost being. You knit me together in my mother's womb. I will give thanks to you, for I am fearfully and wonderfully made. Your works are wonderful. My soul knows that very well. My frame wasn't hidden from you, when I was made in secret, woven together in the depths of the earth. Your eyes saw my body. In your book they were all written, the days that were ordained for me, when as yet there were none of them. How precious to me are your thoughts, God! How vast is their sum!" (Psalms 139:13-17)

I am wonderfully and fearfully made! One of the little sayings I use all the time is when people ask me "how are you?" I tell them, "I'm wonderfully and fearfully made, I just can't figure out why God was skeer'd!"

---

18 "God and Astronomers" (1978) p. 116

70

That's what the Bible says about me. That's what the Bible says about you. We are wonderfully and fearfully made. Those are the words used in the Scriptures. Wonderfully and fearfully. A lot of people try to answer my question when I say that I don't know what God was skeer'd of me. They point out that God isn't afraid of anything! But I'm not one of those people that try to tell you that the Scripture says one thing but actually means another, that every single English translation for the last 400 years has been wrong. I am quite certain that the people entrusted to translate Scriptures know a lot more about the languages they are translating than I ever will.

Here is what I do know. I know how to speak and use the English language. And more importantly, I know how to use a dictionary! So rather than try to translate the word יֵרֵא "yaw-ray" from Hebrew into English, which, incidentally according to Strong's Concordance means, "to fear; morally to revere;" I decided to trust two things: 1) to trust that since the majority of translations of Psalm 139:14 over the last 400 years uses the word, "fearfully", that it's probably a safe bet that's the word God intended and 2) That God is quite capable of preserving His own Word. So I opened my trusty dictionary and looked up the word "fearfully."

The word "fearfully" has two primary definitions: feeling fear, dread, apprehension. Examples would be "fearful for his life; fearful lest he commits suicide."

The second primary definition is this: full of awe or reverence.

I got to thinking about this earlier this morning. My first reaction is that the context would indicate the second definition, "full of awe or reverence", and according to Strong's Concordance, this is indeed the meaning intended in the text; but, when I get into it a bit deeper, God knew before He even created us that He would send His Son to die for us, so all the while He was creating us, He was indeed "fearful for his life" because He knew the consequence to Himself for creating us. Talk about awe and reverence!

While reading through Genesis, note that man was the final creation. God had already created everything there is. Before God began creating man, He took counsel with Himself, "God said, 'Let Us make man in our image, in our likeness'" (Genesis 1:26). This is not an explicit revelation of the Trinity but is part of the foundation for such, as God reveals an "us" within the Godhead. God makes the man, and man is made in the image of God (men and women both bear His image) and is special above all other creatures. To emphasize this, God places man in authority over the earth and over all the other creatures. God blesses man and commands him to reproduce, fill the earth and subdue it (bring it under the rightful stewardship of man as authorized by God).

How can we think less of ourselves when God is in awe of us? Not only is God in awe of us, but He also LOVES us. The most familiar verse of Scripture in the New Testament is John 3:16.

> For God SO loved the world that He gave His only begotten Son, that whoever believes in Him shall not perish, but have eternal life.

That is one powerful verse of Scripture. God SO loved the world. That word, SO, is HUGE! I often say that the word "SO" in John 3:16 is the biggest word in the whole Bible and for certain it's the biggest adverb.

That word is οὕτως "hoo-toos" in Greek. It literally means "in this manner." I'm not going to translate the Scriptures with a Hebrew/Greek/English dictionary. I'm going to trust that the translators know more about it than I do and trust that God intended that to be the word. So I looked up the word "SO" in my dictionary just to make sure I understand English. Check this out:

1. in the way or manner indicated, described, or implied: Do it so.

2. to the extent or degree indicated or suggested: Do not walk so fast.
3. in such a manner, as to follow or result from: As he learned, so did he teach.

For God SO loved the world. In what manner did He love the world? He loved it enough to sacrifice his one and only Son for us. Every time the New Testament speaks of God's love, it's always in a demonstration.

"By this, we know love, because he laid down his life for us. And we ought to lay down our lives for the brothers." (1 John 3:16)

"But God commends his own love toward us, in that while we were yet sinners, Christ died for us." (Romans 5:8)

It doesn't read, …when we turned away from our wicked ways, Christ died for us… It doesn't read, …when we cleaned up our act, Christ died for us… The value God places upon us is His own life.

Jesus said Greater love has no one than this than to lay down one's life for his friends. (John 15:13 NKJV)

What are any of us worth? God thinks we are worth dying for. *We are worth dying for.!*

Chapter Ten
Discovering God

When a Russian cosmonaut returned from space and reported that he had not found God, C.S. Lewis responded that this was like Hamlet going into the attic of his castle looking for Shakespeare. If there is a God, He wouldn't be another object in the universe that could be put in a lab and analyzed with empirical methods. He would relate to us the way a playwright relates to the characters in his play. We (the characters) might be able to know quite a lot about the playwright, but only to the degree, the author chooses to put information about himself into the play.[19]

How we know and experience God is limited by what we can perceive through our five senses. The issue with that is that we cannot see, taste, smell, hear, or touch God (at least not directly in the physical sense). An analogy I've heard before to describe our experience with God is that you can't see the wind, but you know what the wind is by what it does. You can see the effects of the wind; you can hear the roar of the wind, feel the wind touch against your body, smell scents from other places because of the wind bringing them to you, and I suppose if something blows into your mouth, you can taste it too!

The Bible states:

"For the invisible things of him since the creation of the world are clearly seen, being perceived through the

---

19 Timothy Keller, *The Reason For God.,* p. 122 © 2008 Timothy Keller. Published by Dutton

things that are made, even his everlasting power and divinity; that they may be without excuse." (Romans 1:20)

We can see the evidence of God through observing His creation. Much discussion and debate have come about from trying to explain creation. Hardliners for both Creationism and for Evolution can argue for eternity about the issue. Even Darwin suggested in 1859 that there must be a *First Cause* to get evolution going.[20]

First Cause is the concept that everything we can observe must have something to cause it to happen. While it's feasible that events can go on indefinitely into the future, it does not make sense that the causes can go infinitely into the past. At some point, something caused the events that come after. This concept was first developed by Aristotle and then later enhanced by Aquinas.

I stated in the last chapter that one could not deny the existence of a god, but we can disagree about who or what he is. What is interesting to me is that we have so many ideas about who and what God is. The Apostle says that God's eternal power and divine nature have been clearly seen, but even amongst people that claim the same belief system in the same congregation of the same religion, an agreement cannot be reached. I was talking to someone the other day about some of the differences in doctrine we have. Both of us claim to use the Bible as our guide, yet, we have some very different understandings of God, His will, and His nature. We are of different "denominations." Denominal differences in our understanding of doctrine might partially explain things, but my friend then began telling me about another church bearing the same denomination as his had split away from his church assembly over doctrinal differences. The one congregation

---

20 Darwin Correspondence Project – Letter 8837 – Darwin, C. R. to Doedes, N. D., 2 Apr 1873". Retrieved 19 November 2008.

takes the liberal view of doctrine. The one he is associated with takes a more hardline one.

There's the story about the man that was rescued from a deserted island. After he had returned to civilization, he was asked by a news crew to go back to the island and do a story about life on the island. When they got to the island, the man showed them 3 huts. He told them, the first one was my house, it's where I lived the entire time I lived on the island. The second hut was my church. The third hut was the new church I built after I got mad at the preacher in the other hut!

I'm fascinated at how many interpretations of the Scriptures there are. There are entire disciplines of study devoted to different doctrines in the Bible. Origins Theology, the discussion of Creation Science; Eschatology, study of End times & Prophecy; Soteriology, the theological doctrine of salvation; Dispensationalism, the discussion of dispensationalist theology; Paterology, Christology & Pneumatology the doctrine & nature of God the Father, Christ the Son & the Holy Spirit; Hamartiology, doctrine of sin, the origin of sin and how sin entered into the world, just to name a very few! My fascination leads me to some pretty interesting and often intense "discussions" about different doctrines

A recently baptized friend asked me Sunday, "what do we believe about baptizing infants?" My answer surprised him. I said, "there is no what do 'we' believe. What do you believe?" That took him back because no one had ever invited him to contemplate anything on his own. Like so many of us, he had been content to believe what someone else tells him to believe. Unfortunately, no one ever taught him how to seek God himself.

I firmly believe it is necessary to question my beliefs. I think the results of examining what I believe are twofold:

1) To confirm the Truth of what I already believe; or,
2) To debunk what I believe, which brings me closer to Truth.

The Bible teaches us to seek God:

> "But from there you shall seek Yahweh your God, and you shall find him when you search after him with all your heart and with all your soul." (Deuteronomy 4:29)

> "You shall seek me, and find me when you search for me with all your heart." (Jerimiah 29:13)

The Scriptures teach us to search with our souls and heart. He says if we seek Him, we will find Him.
Jesus taught us:

> "However when he, the Spirit of truth, has come, he will guide you into all truth, for he will not speak from himself; but whatever he hears, he will speak. He will declare to you things that are coming." (John 16:13)

And that the Holy Spirit resides in the believer:

> "the Spirit of truth, whom the world can't receive; for it doesn't see him, neither knows him. You know him, for he lives with you, and will be in you." (John 14:17)

He lives with you and will be in you. ...IN YOU... I looked that verse up on multiple translations, and in every one of them, it reads, *in you!* How far do we need to look for God if He is IN us?

Now, while it's true that God has equipped the church with apostles, prophets, evangelists, pastors, and teachers,[21] we are not to rely wholly on them. We are to seek God with our own heart and soul, not to have someone else seek God and then tell us about Him! If anything, we are to question what others teach us about God. Paul once applauded a group for researching what he taught them.

---

21 Ephesians 4:11

"Now these were nobler than those in Thessalonica, in that they received the word with all readiness of mind, examining the Scriptures daily to see whether these things were so." (Acts 17:11)

One of my pastor's laments is that so many people have become complacent in their spirituality. Many roam from church to church looking to get "fed." He says that if the only time you eat is once or twice a week, you're going to starve. Too many of us are content to have someone else spoon-feed us the Truth about God rather than consult with Him ourselves by studying His Word and spending time with Him in prayer and meditation.

The way I seek to know and understand God is to study the Bible; not only the text but also commentaries and word studies. The main reason for reading commentaries is for the historical and cultural knowledge gained from the scriptures. Knowing the culture of the society that existed in Biblical times really brings the language and expressions used in the translations alive, and often brings a clearer understanding to the words I am reading. I also tend to read multiple translations. There are some who disagree with that concept (taking their preference for any particular translation to the point of idolatry), but when you do word studies on any passage of Scripture, you will see how many different ways any individual sentence can be translated. My usual choices for studying a passage of Scripture are NKJV, NASB, ESV, and NRSV. In my library are 20+ other translations and on my computer, I have 17 translations (http://e-sword.net). I've used many different methods of studying over the years. My current study is to do "Bible in a year" with The Listener's Bible (http://listenersbible.com/devotionals/biy/) and then throughout the day read whatever I feel led to read (currently Hosea & Ezekiel), and whenever something I'm reading gives me something to ponder, I stop and sit quietly for a while and meditate on what I just read. Countless epiphanies have occurred during these times that are confirmed over and over in the days immediately thereafter.

C.S. Lewis was correct when he stated that looking for God in space was like Hamlet looking for Shakespeare in the attic of his castle. Hamlet can only know what Shakespeare wrote into the play for Hamlet to know. God has written Himself into our world in the form of His Son, Jesus. If we want to know the nature of God, all we have to do is look at Jesus. The only way we can do that is to read His book (Bible) and spend time with Him. It's one thing to have me tell you how great God is. It's quite another for you to experience it yourself.

Chapter Eleven
Hiding From God

My 3 and 4-year-old daughters tend to wake up significantly earlier than my wife, and I do. Each morning as we hear them stirring, we start the process of getting up ourselves. However, the toddlers wake up running full tilt on 10 of a 10 scale, and we wake up about a 2 of 10 needing a coffee or three to get to 6 or 7. There is usually a gap of time between the girls getting up and us getting up. It's AMAZING what toddlers can get into in 10-20 minutes.

Amazing.

Take this morning as an example. The girls were up about 5:15 AM when we heard them. Rachel and I took turns telling each other that it's your turn to get up with the girls. That went on for a while and finally, we start stirring and getting out of bed. As soon as my feet hit the floor and the girls knew we were getting up, the atmosphere of the entire house changed. They started running and then got very quiet. Extremely quiet.

At that moment I knew I wasn't going to be happy with what I found. They knew I wasn't going to be happy with what I found. My darling precious, adorable daughters heard their daddy stir and immediately went into hiding.

I walked out of my bedroom and immediately noticed the sea that was once my kitchen. I say sea because as I further investigated, I found that any place not covered with water was covered in the salt they had dumped out of the shakers so they could fill the shakers with water. Then I looked in the living room. The sea continued, but this sea was polluted with whatever leftover drinks we left from last night. I found a bowl with what looked like Coke in it…. Anyway, as you can imagine, I was pretty upset. I'm toning it down here while we talk, but I was upset!

I YELLED for the girls to come out. Anyone in our house or any of the houses surrounding our house were now awake. The girls, fearing my wrath, understandably didn't come out right away. When I finally do see them, I'm screaming at them, "who did this?" "Why did you do this?...etc. "Why can't I wake up one morning without finding everything in the house destroyed?"

You get the idea.

My precious princesses had done evil in my sight, and they knew it. They knew when they were doing it it was wrong and that I would be very upset. Why else would they have scrambled and hidden at the first hint that I had gotten up?

> "Now the serpent was more subtle than any animal of the field which Yahweh God had made. He said to the woman, "Has God really said, 'You shall not eat of any tree of the garden'?" The woman said to the serpent, "We may eat fruit from the trees of the garden, but not the fruit of the tree which is in the middle of the garden. God has said, 'You shall not eat of it. You shall not touch it, lest you die.'" The serpent said to the woman, "You won't really die, for God knows that in the day you eat it, your eyes will be opened, and you will be like God, knowing good and evil." When the woman saw that the tree was good for food, and that it was a delight to the eyes, and that the tree was to be desired to make one wise, she took some of its fruit, and ate; and she gave some to her husband with her, and he ate it, too. Their eyes were opened, and they both knew that they were naked. They sewed fig leaves together and made coverings for themselves. They heard Yahweh God's voice walking in the garden in the cool of the day, and the man and his wife hid from the presence of Yahweh God among the trees of the garden. Yahweh God called

to the man, and said to him, "Where are you?" The man said, "I heard your voice in the garden, and I was afraid because I was naked, and I hid." God said, "Who told you that you were naked? Have you eaten from the tree that I commanded you not to eat from?" The man said, "The woman whom you gave to be with me, she gave me fruit from the tree, and I ate it." Yahweh God said to the woman, "What have you done?" The woman said, "The serpent deceived me, and I ate." (Genesis 3:1-13)

Most everyone is familiar with this particular Bible story. Let's take a moment to look at the parallels between what the Scripture recounts here and what I just told you about this morning. Both Adam and Eve knew they weren't supposed to eat from the Tree of Knowledge. They had been given free rein to eat from ANY OTHER TREE sans the ONE. How often are we like that in God's kingdom? We are just like little children. The Bible even describes us as children.

"The Spirit himself testifies with our spirit that we are children of God; and if children, then heirs; heirs of God, and joint-heirs with Christ; if indeed we suffer with him, that we may also be glorified with him." (Romans 8:16-17)

We are children of God. We are joint heirs with the Son of God, Christ Jesus. We can look out at the garden and realize that we can eat from any of a multitude of trees and plants, but instead of looking at all we can have and enjoy, we look to that one thing we can't have.

My children have more toys than they will ever be able to play with, but rather than play with what they are supposed to play with, they dump the salt shakers on the floor and fill them with water from the sink.

In this same manner, Adam and Eve made a conscious decision to disobey God. That's an important distinction to make. People want to say "the devil made me do it," but the devil doesn't have that kind of power. All he can do is suggest things to us, to lie to us, but he cannot make us do anything.

They heard the sound of the LORD God walking in the garden in the cool of the day. "The sound of the Lord." You ever wonder what that is? The "sound of the Lord"? The word translated "sound" here is translated "voice" in the New King James Version. It's the Hebrew word, קוֹל qol (phonetically: kole). Like so many words in any language, it can literally have many different meanings and we have to look at the context to determine the correct translation.

> From an unused root meaning to call aloud; a voice or sound: - + aloud, bleating, crackling, cry (+ out), fame, lightness, lowing, noise, + hold peace, [pro-] claim, proclamation, + sing, sound, + spark, thunder (-ing), voice, + yell.

At least 3 other times in the Scriptures קוֹל is translated "thunder" to describe the voice of the Lord:

> "Listen closely to the thunder of His voice, And the rumbling that goes out from His mouth." (Job 37:2 NASB)

> "You called in trouble, and I delivered you; I answered you in the secret place of thunder; I tested you at the waters of Meribah. Selah" (Psalms 81:7 NKJV)

> "The LORD thundered from heaven, And the Most High uttered His voice, Hailstones, and coals of fire." (Psalms 18:13 NKJV)

When the LORD gave the 10 commandments to Moses on Mount Sinai, the Israelites heard thunder from the mountain.

That's what my toddlers heard when they heard my foot touch down on the wooden floors of our house. They heard the thunder that would be their father coming to see what they had done!

Next, in the narrative, we hear God call out to Adam and Eve. "Where are you?" Are we to believe that the omnipresent God of the Universe didn't know where the two were at? Again, to parallel this morning, I knew exactly where the girls were. They had run and hid in their room. Olivia hides behind the changing table next to the closet, and Sophia hides behind the dresser next to her bed. Knowing exactly where they were, I asked them where they are. Then, knowing what they had done, I did just like God in the story and asked them what they'd done. Then just like Adam and Eve, Olivia and Sophia tried to blame each other or even me for what had just happened. So it is when we do something wrong. More often than not, we know we are doing something that doesn't please God.

"My son, don't forget my teaching; but let your heart keep my commandments: for length of days, and years of life, and peace, they will add to you. Don't let kindness and truth forsake you. Bind them around your neck. Write them on the tablet of your heart. So you will find favor and good understanding in the sight of God and man. Trust in Yahweh with all your heart, and don't lean on your own understanding. In all your ways acknowledge him, and he will make your paths straight. Don't be wise in your own eyes. Fear Yahweh, and depart from evil. It will be health to your body, and nourishment to your bones. Honor Yahweh with your substance, with the first fruits of all your increase: so your barns will be filled with plenty, and your vats will overflow with new wine. My son, don't despise Yahweh's discipline, neither be weary of his reproof: for whom Yahweh loves, he reproves; even as a father reproves the son in whom he delights." (Proverbs 3:1-12)

Adam and Eve sinned. When they became aware of what they had done, they tried to cover up their nakedness themselves by sewing together some fig leaves. The leaves covered their bodies but didn't cover their sin. Fact is, we can't cover up our sins from God. But something interesting happens in the Adam and Eve story. After all the sin, shame, trying to deal with it themselves, getting caught, and then being disciplined, In verse 21 it reads that God made coverings for them out of animal skins and clothed them. Through it all, God is the one that provides the cover for sin.

The fact is that God already knows what we are going to do even before we actually do it. Hiding doesn't do any good. His discipline is designed to correct our behavior and bring us closer to Him. Just like in the Garden of Eden, God will be the one doing the covering. The animal skins used in Genesis 3 are a shadow of what was to come.

> "For the wages of sin is death, but the free gift of God is eternal life in Christ Jesus our Lord." (Romans 6:23)

In Leviticus, we read that "the life is in the blood."[22] The price for Adam's sin had to be paid. The price is paid with a life. The blood of the animals sacrificed for Adam and Eve's sin covered a specific sin. The problem is the blood of animals is not a long-term solution. That's why the Hebrews had a system for sacrificing animals over and over again for their sins. The covering in Genesis 3 is a shadow of what was to come.

From the Book of Hebrews:

> "For the law, having a shadow of the good to come, not the very image of the things, can never with the same sacrifices year by year, which they offer continually, make perfect those who draw near. Or else wouldn't they have ceased to be offered, because the worshipers,

---

22 Leviticus 17:11

having been once cleansed, would have had no more consciousness of sins? But in those sacrifices, there is a yearly reminder of sins. For it is impossible that the blood of bulls and goats should take away sins. Therefore, when he comes into the world, he says, "Sacrifice and offering you didn't desire, but you prepared a body for me. You had no pleasure in whole burnt offerings and sacrifices for sin. Then I said, 'Behold, I have come (in the scroll of the book it is written of me) to do your will, O God.'" Previously saying, "Sacrifices and offerings and whole burnt offerings and sacrifices for sin you didn't desire, neither had pleasure in them" (those which are offered according to the law), then he has said, "Behold, I have come to do your will." He takes away the first that he may establish the second, by which will we have been sanctified through the offering of the body of Jesus Christ once for all. Every priest indeed stands day by day serving and often offering the same sacrifices, which can never take away sins, but he, when he had offered one sacrifice for sins forever, sat down on the right hand of God; from that time waiting until his enemies are made the footstool of his feet. For by one offering he has perfected forever those who are being sanctified. The Holy Spirit also testifies to us, for after saying, "This is the covenant that I will make with them: 'After those days,' says the Lord, 'I will put my laws on their heart, I will also write them on their mind;'" then he says, "I will remember their sins and their iniquities no more." Now where remission of these is, there is no more offering for sin." (Hebrews 10:1-18)

Coming full circle to where this teaching came from, here from Psalm 139:

"For the Chief Musician. A Psalm by David. Yahweh, you have searched me, and you know me. You know my sitting down and my rising up. You perceive my thoughts from afar. You search out my path and my lying down and are acquainted with all my ways. For there is not a word on my tongue, but, behold, Yahweh, you know it altogether. You hem me in behind and before. You laid your hand on me. This knowledge is beyond me. It's lofty. I can't attain it. Where could I go from your Spirit? Or where could I flee from your presence? If I ascend up into heaven, you are there. If I make my bed in Sheol, behold, you are there! If I take the wings of the dawn, and settle in the uttermost parts of the sea; Even there your hand will lead me, and your right hand will hold me." (Psalms 139:1-10)

The part that strikes me to the core is the statement, *If I make my bed in Sheol, {hell in other translations} behold, you are there!* Either one can be in awe of the omnipresence of God, or one can be scared of the fact God is *everywhere*.

Chapter Twelve
I Have To Be Poor?

I am constantly amused by how our Western culture has reshaped Christianity into some sort of all my troubles are gone feel-good religion. Jesus never promised us a physical life devoid of disappointments and turmoil, if anything, He promises us the opposite.

> And he said to all, "If anyone would come after me, let him deny himself and take up his cross daily and follow me. For whoever would save his life will lose it, but whoever loses his life for my sake will save it. (Luke 9:23-24 ESV)

On this side of history, we understand this passage because we know that Jesus was crucified on a cross. But, Jesus said this *before* the crucifixion and before any of His followers understood that He would one day go to the cross on our behalf. I imagine today He would say, "If anyone would come after Me, let him deny himself and take up a lethal injection daily and come follow Me." What the people heard in this message and understood is that the cross was a device for producing death.

Crucifixion was the cruelest and most humiliating way the Romans could come up with to kill a person. It is so heinous Roman citizens couldn't legally be put to death in that manner. Roman orator Cicero said:

> To bind a Roman citizen is a crime, to flog him is an abomination, to kill him is almost an act of murder:

to crucify him is -- What? There is no fitting word
that can possibly describe so horrible a deed."[23]

Crucifixion was not only designed as capital punishment; it
serves as a warning to any that would question the power of
Rome. Most victims of crucifixion were left hanging on their
crosses until they literally rotted off or were eaten by animals.
This was to warn others of the consequences of going against
the wishes of Rome.

Most often this passage is used to teach us that we are to
"die to self" in order to be alive in Christ. What that means, to
be "alive in Christ" is another entirely different teaching.

"Don't look for shortcuts to God. The market is flooded
with surefire, easygoing formulas for a successful life
that can be practiced in your spare time. Don't fall for
that stuff, even though crowds of people do. The way to
life—to God!—is vigorous and requires total attention.
(Matthew 7:13-14 MSG)

I quoted *The Message* there because I personally believe the
contemporary language is significantly easier to understand
than the more traditional reading:

"Enter in by the narrow gate; for wide is the gate and
broad is the way that leads to destruction, and many are
those who enter in by it. How narrow is the gate, and
restricted is the way that leads to life! Few are those who
find it." (Matthew 7:13-14)

The gentleman that wrote most of the New Testament,
Paul of Tarsus, who was called by God to be an Apostle, lived

---

23 *Stott, John R. (1986). The Cross of Christ. InterVarsity Press.
p. 24.* **ISBN 0-87784-998-6**. (citing Cicero, Against Verres II.v.66,
para. 170)

one tragedy after another. Following the Holy Spirit, he experienced quite a bit of persecution. He writes:

> "Are they servants of Christ? (I speak as one beside himself) I am more so; in labors more abundantly, in prisons more abundantly, in stripes above measure, in deaths often. Five times from the Jews I received forty stripes minus one. Three times I was beaten with rods. Once I was stoned. Three times I suffered shipwreck. I have been a night and a day in the deep. I have been in travels often, perils of rivers, perils of robbers, perils from my countrymen, perils from the Gentiles, perils in the city, perils in the wilderness, perils in the sea, perils among false brothers; in labor and travail, in watchings often, in hunger and thirst, in fastings often, and in cold and nakedness. Besides those things that are outside, there is that which presses on me daily: anxiety for all the assemblies." (2 Corinthians 11:23-28)

Jesus' followers also are not promised that we will receive everything we think we want when we want if only we pray for it "in Jesus' name." It is true that He said:

> "Whatever you will ask in my name, I will do it, that the Father may be glorified in the Son. If you ask anything in my name, I will do it." (John 14:13-14)

However, that cannot mean using the incantation "in Jesus' name" magically makes something happen. If so, we'd be no more than magicians. To speak "in the name of" means to speak with the authority of that person. "STOP! In the name of the law!" is a great example. The law enforcement officer has the authority of "the law" to issue that command. Foreign ambassadors are another example. Ambassadors to other countries from the United States have the authority to speak as if they were speaking on behalf of the President.

Later on, Jesus goes on to explain this in the Book of John:

"If you remain in me, and my words remain in you, you will ask whatever you desire, and it will be done for you. "In this is my Father glorified, that you bear much fruit; and so you will be my disciples." (John 15:7-8)

To pray in Jesus' name is to pray according to HIS will, not our own. If whatever we are asking isn't in His will, then we aren't really asking in His name and authority. Jesus' will for us is eternal life. He defines it in John 17:3

"This is eternal life, that they should know you, the only true God, and him whom you sent, Jesus Christ." (John 17:3)

God promises to be with us always and forever. Forever is an amazingly long time. We get caught up in things that are temporal (temporary), but God is mostly concerned with eternity. We focus on today and maybe tomorrow. We focus on what we need. What we want. The problem with all that is, for the most part, nothing we do or accomplish will be remembered two generations from now (go on, name your great-grandfathers on your mother's or father's side!) As Solomon wrote in Ecclesiastes,

"What does man gain from all his labor in which he labors under the sun? One generation goes, and another generation comes, but the earth remains forever. The sun also rises, and the sun goes down and hurries to its place where it rises. The wind goes toward the south and turns around to the north. It turns around continually as it goes, and the wind returns again to its courses. All the rivers run into the sea, yet the sea is not full. To the place where the rivers flow, there they flow again. All things are full of weariness beyond uttering. The eye is not satisfied with seeing, nor the ear filled with hearing. That which has been is that which shall be; and that which has been done is that which shall be done: and there is no new thing under the sun. Is there a thing of which it may be said, "Behold, this is new?" It has been long ago, in the ages which were before us. There is no memory of the former; neither shall there be any memory of the latter that are to come, among those that shall come after." (Ecclesiastes 1:3-11)

The Christian's life is only fulfilling when they focus primarily on Him and let everything else be temporal. Paul writes of being content at all times.

I rejoiced in the Lord greatly that now at length you have revived your concern for me. You were indeed concerned for me, but you had no opportunity. Not that I am speaking of being in need, for I have learned in whatever situation I am to be content. I know how to be brought low, and I know how to abound. In any and every circumstance, I have learned the secret of facing plenty and hunger, abundance and need. I can do all things through him who strengthens me. (Philippians 4:10-13)

None of this means that God desires or intends us to be *poor*. Many theologians throughout history have interpreted the Scriptures to imply that it is more pious to be poor and there are even sects of believers that take a vow of poverty thinking that somehow this will make them closer to God. I read somewhere earlier today someone quoting this Scripture:

"Again I tell you, it is easier for a camel to go through a needle's eye, than for a rich man to enter into God's Kingdom." (Matthew 19:24)

On the surface, out of context, and taken to its extreme logical conclusion I can see where someone could come to the conclusion that being rich is bad and being poor is good. However, Jesus was using an *aphorism*. An aphorism is a concise, terse, laconic, and/or memorable expression of a general truth or principle. A modern American English aphorism would be, "If it ain't broke, don't fix it." Another example would be, "Power tends to corrupt, and absolute power corrupts absolutely" (Lord Acton). Jesus was using a Hebrew expression that had been around for eons. This idiom is used in both the Babylonian Talmud and the Midrash. In the Talmud, it's used to describe a man's dreams. However, I believe Jesus was referencing the Midrash:

> A Midrash on the *Song of Songs* uses the phrase to speak of God's willingness and ability beyond comparison, to accomplish the salvation of a sinner:

> The Holy One said, open for me a door as big as a needle's eye and I will open for you a door through which may enter tents and camels?[24]

In context and knowing the idiom Jesus was using, it isn't *impossible* for the rich man to get to heaven, just very difficult because the rich man valued his possessions more than he valued following the Lord. Using this phrase, He was again stating that only God can make way for mankind to be redeemed.

Another pair of verses that gets used to justify poverty and make one closer to God :

> "Blessed are the poor in spirit, for theirs is the Kingdom of Heaven." (Matthew 5:3)

---

24 'The camel and the eye of the needle', Matthew 19:24, Mark 10:25, Luke 18:25". Hebrew New Testament Studies. Retrieved 21 June 2011.

> "He lifted up his eyes to his disciples, and said, "Blessed are you who are poor, God's Kingdom is yours." (Luke 6:20)

English theologian Charles J. Ellicott had this to say about these two verses:

> The poor in spirit.—The limitation, as in "the pure in heart," points to the region of life in which the poverty is found. In Luke 6:20 there is no such qualifying clause, and there the words speak of outward poverty, as in itself a less perilous and therefore happier state than that of riches. Here the blessedness is that of those who, whatever their outward state may be, are in their inward life as those who feel that they have nothing of their own, must be receivers before they give, must be dependent on another's bounty, and be, as it were, the "bedesmen" {a person that prays out of a sense of duty} of the great King. To that temper of mind belongs the "kingdom of heaven," the eternal realities, in this life and the life to come, of that society of which Christ is the Head. Things are sometimes best understood by their contraries, and we may point to the description of the church of Laodicea as showing us the opposite type of character, thinking itself "rich" in the spiritual life when it is really as "the pauper," destitute of the true riches, blind and naked.

Having wealth isn't a sin nor is it something to prevent one from entering the Kingdom of Heaven. Wealth, whether it be money or land or livestock is just stuff. There are plenty of promises in the Bible that people with faith will prosper and have more than they could ever want or need. The problem isn't the stuff; it's when we put obtaining wealth and prosperity before our relationship with God. It's an attitude problem. This brings us back to the whole "dying to self" verses. We

DANNY B. POWELL

should be thankful when we have things, but we should be more thankful that we are called sons of God.

Chapter Thirteen
The Most Toys WINS!

Back in 2008, I tracked all the news about the Bear-Stearns collapse and subsequent bail-out with great enthusiasm. I haven't yet decided how I feel about the way the United States government responded. On the one hand, the decision of the Federal Reserve to back $30,000,000,000.00 of the suspect (read "bad") loans with U.S. tax dollars probably averted at least momentarily a deep recession in the United States if not the entire world. Had Bear-Stearns been allowed to go bankrupt, billions of dollars of monetary transactions (in progress) that they oversaw would have been frozen indefinitely by a bankruptcy court. Many people don't realize that banks like Bear-Stearns handle millions of financial transactions for smaller banks on a daily basis. Grandma and grandpa's mutual fund might have been locked up to the point they couldn't get any of their money out for a decade or longer even if that mutual fund wasn't directly managed by Bear-Stearns. Every one of those transactions would have been frozen while the courts sorted it out. Then in addition to Bear-Stearns failing, other banks that have leveraged themselves with loans that should have never been made would have begun falling like the proverbial dominos. On this hand, the moves by our government appear to be the right thing to do.

This subject has been near and dear to my heart because I am one of those people that have had a suspect (read "bad") loan. I didn't have a sub-prime mortgage on a home, but I did have an incredibly high-interest loan on my car. What makes the loan suspect (again, read, "bad") is that at one point I owed nearly $5,000.00 more on the car than what I could reasonably expect to pay for the exact same vehicle from someone else. The common term for this is that I am "upside down" in my loan. If you're not familiar with how this works, let me briefly explain it.

At the time I took out the first loan, I was making only $1600.00 a month (before taxes) GMAC decided it was a good idea to give me a $15,000.00 loan on a Nissan pickup. With the insurance that I was required to have on the truck, my payment was almost $500 a month. At $16,00.00 a month, my take-home pay was slightly more than $300 a week. I also paid over $700.00 a month for rent and utilities, and I had a wife and baby to support. It doesn't take a rocket scientist to realize that I really couldn't afford that loan. The loan was for 4 years.

Three and a half years into that loan, for whatever reason, I needed to have a new truck. I still owed almost $2,000 on the truck I was trading in on the new truck. NO PROBLEM! The finance company (this time Ford Motor Credit) just tacks on the payoff of the last loan onto the new one. This time the great deal I got was 36 payments of $525.00 a month plus insurance (total about $700.00 a month). (You'll want to read this next sentence with a tone of extreme sarcasm.) The best part was the $8,352.00 balloon payment at the end of the 36 months. As you can well imagine, I didn't have the payoff nor had I been able to maintain timely payments for 36 months, so Ford Motor Company Credit wasn't really interested in refinancing the balance on the truck.

Again, *NO PROBLEM!* I walked into another car dealer, told them my dilemma, and an hour later I drove off the lot in a brand new car. The $8,352.00 was just added to my new note. The only "good part" of the new loan is that the payments are about $150.00 a month less than what I was paying out. Now I feel like I'm still paying for that first truck I bought and I actually see the last truck I traded every day when I pick my son up from school each day and realize that I'm paying for that truck AND the person driving it now is paying for it.

In addition to the whole loan situation that exists both in automobiles (like what I'm doing) and giving loans to folks for new homes that can't afford them, I've discovered there are entire industries aimed at lower-income people. Here's the part that angers me: the less you can afford something, the more it costs! Lower income people pay more for banking (you have to have minimum balances in order to get free checking), higher interest rates for credit, higher prices for durable goods on credit (price anything at a "rent to own store" sometime) and outrageous fees for banking related services such as check cashing and debit cards.

Anecdotally it appears that our culture and society intends to keep people in poverty. Our entire culture is driven by the consumption of goods. I constantly think that I need new things. I quit getting credit cards because I'd always get them "for emergencies only" yet they'd always be charged to the maximum within 90 days because of all the "emergencies" I'd have.

Whose fault is it? I was discussing this with one of my good friends at church a week ago. He said, "Do you blame the kid who eats all the candy or the person who put the bowl right in front of him?"

I'd been trying to write this chapter for a few weeks but couldn't seem ever to get started. While in the process of getting this to the computer, my pastor started doing a series of life lessons called "Adventures in Missing the Point" which is loosely based on the book by the same title by Brian D. McLaren and Tony Campolo. After a couple of the lessons, I picked up a copy of the book for myself.

If you knew me back in 2008, you knew that eschatology (the study of end times) was not my favorite subject. If anything, I told people I didn't really care how it all ends. I really didn't because I already knew how it ends. However, having said that, the first adventure in missing the point I read in the book was missing the point of end times. I never cease to be amazed at how God works in my life. For one thing, Campolo's eschatology is incredibly similar to what mine was at the time. That intrigued me to the point that I wanted to read more of the chapter. Then he gets to the part that applies to exactly what's been on my mind for the last few weeks. Right there in the 17th chapter of Revelations, it talks about Babylon.

"The woman was dressed in purple and scarlet, and decked with gold and precious stones and pearls, having in her hand a golden cup full of abominations and the impurities of the sexual immorality of the earth. And on her forehead, a name was written, "MYSTERY, BABYLON THE GREAT, THE MOTHER OF THE PROSTITUTES AND OF THE ABOMINATIONS OF THE EARTH." I saw the woman drunken with the blood of the saints, and with the blood of the martyrs of Jesus. When I saw her, I wondered with great amazement." (Revelation 17:4-6)

The first century Christians understood that "Babylon" was code for the Roman Empire. It was code for the society in which the Christian lives in. This is an understanding that we can apply to the Scriptures today. Our culture and society are our Babylon, the "Great Whore." And like any great whore, she encourages us to live way beyond our means and bring us to our knees in an effort to get more and more.

The Bible continues by telling us that great Babylon will fall and calls for Believers to come out of Babylon while they still can:

"He cried with a mighty voice, saying, "Fallen, fallen is Babylon the great, and she has become a habitation of demons, a prison of every unclean spirit, and a prison of every unclean and hateful bird! For all the nations have drunk of the wine of the wrath of her sexual immorality, the kings of the earth committed sexual immorality with her, and the merchants of the earth grew rich from the abundance of her luxury." I heard another voice from heaven, saying, "Come out of her, my people, that you have no participation in her sins, and that you don't receive of her plagues, for her sins have reached to the

sky, and God has remembered her
iniquities." (Revelation 18:2-5)

If you are questioning whether our culture and society is our
Babylon, look at this description in the 18th chapter of
Revelations:

"And the merchants of the earth will weep and mourn
over her, for no one buys their merchandise anymore:
merchandise of gold and silver, precious stones and
pearls, fine linen and purple, silk and scarlet, every kind
of citron wood, every kind of object of ivory, every kind
of object of most precious wood, bronze, iron, and
marble; and cinnamon and incense, fragrant oil and
frankincense, wine and oil, fine flour and wheat, cattle
and sheep, horses and chariots, and bodies and souls of
men. (Revelation 18:11-13 NKJV)

Shop till you drop! The one who dies with the most toys wins!
    This brings me to "the other hand" about how I feel about
our government's actions regarding the Bear-Stearns situation.
The Bible says that the saints will rejoice when Babylon falls. I
know I will. While it would have annoyed me to no end to have
been denied that first car loan, looking back at it now I realize
that the bank had no real business loaning it to me, nor did I
have any business taking out that loan. I could have purchased
a good used car or truck for significantly less money. I
especially wish now that I had been denied credit on that
second truck!
    It took me a long time to let go of the entire situation
(close to a decade!). For the longest time, if it weren't for the
fact that many good individuals would have to suffer because
of the greed of the banks and merchants that fuel the economic
engine of our society, I'd say let the banks that loan money to
people that shouldn't get loans to fail! Let the banks that
foreclose on homes because the loan product they sold can't
be paid back fail! Let the people that invest their monies in

risky subprime loans lose their investments. I have noticed that people that lived during the "Great Depression" have a completely different perspective on money and material things than I do.

Howard Beale in the 1977 movie, Network, said, "I'm as mad as hell, and I'm not going to take it anymore!" In the Revelation of Jesus Christ to John the Apostle we find that after the destruction of Babylon God creates a New Jerusalem. I have come to the realization that I cannot expect to be part of the New Jerusalem if I "share in the sins" of Babylon. I am angry, but I thank GOD that I can see what is happening to me and that with His help, I will break free and join Him in the New Jerusalem.

Chapter Fourteen
Hosea

I am addicted to Facebook. I know that a lot of people I associate with are also addicted because when I log on to Facebook, I chat with them and leave messages on their walls. One of the things that I'm most addicted to is the Facebook quizzes. A term I hear a lot now is *Facebook Official*, meaning that something is true because it was revealed in a Facebook quiz.

One quiz I took was "Which Bible book are you?" I thought I might find that interesting, so I took the quiz. When I got the results I read, "Your result: Hosea":

> You are in touch with the pain of rejection, and this puts you in touch with God. You remain faithful though others do not remain faithful to you. In this way, you are like God, and it is a benefit to you, though it is painful. Because of this experience you have a message to communicate of God's love - and also of the judgment that will come if we refuse to know God.

I found that fascinating at first, but then I realized that it'd been some time since I actually read Hosea, so I didn't really know what this means. I mean, I read my Bible. I read some in it nearly every day, but it's been a really long time since I read any of the Minor Prophets. I have to admit that I've only actually read the entire Bible cover to cover less than a dozen times. The first time was about 25 years ago. I was searching for truth and decided to read it for myself rather than have people explain it to me. The second time was when my son, Zach was a teenager, and we participated in a 12-week Bible study that went through the entire Bible in 12 weeks! If you ever want some real adventure, read the Bible aloud with your teenager. I'll tell you what, parts of it, if it wasn't the Bible, I wouldn't have let him read it! I'm always amused when people tell me "I read the Bible once" and then demonstrate that they have no idea what the book contains.

For any of us not familiar with the Hosea, here is the short version. God tells Hosea to take Gomer, a woman of ill repute to be his bride to illustrate the relationship between God and His chosen people, Israel.

I remember a conversation I had with my wife in the early days of our dating. We were discussing theology when she made the point, "That promise was made to Israel, that doesn't apply to us." Who is God's chosen people, Israel? We have to answer that question first before we can apply anything in Hosea to us Gentile believers today. We say that God is the same today, yesterday, and forever, so if the promises in the Old Testament are made to Israel, we need to know if that applies to us or not.

The New Testament describes believers in Jesus Christ in two different ways. 1) as sons; and, 2) as branches grafted into the root. The way I want to examine is the one concerning branches grafted into the root. In the 53rd chapter of Isaiah, the prophecy concerning the coming Savior describes Him as a root.

> "For he grew up before him as a tender plant, and as a root out of dry ground. He has no good looks or majesty. When we see him, there is no beauty that we should desire him." (Isaiah 53:2)

Jesus then reinforces what Isaiah writes about him when he declares in John 15,

"I am the vine. You are the branches. He who remains in me, and I in him, the same bears much fruit, for apart from me you can do nothing." (John 15:5)

In the 11th chapter of Romans, Paul writes specifically about who Israel is by describing the Israelites that reject Christ as broken off branches and then the Gentile believers as being grafted into the root.

"For I speak to you who are Gentiles. Since then as I am an apostle to Gentiles, I glorify my ministry; if by any means I may provoke to jealousy those who are my flesh and may save some of them. For if the rejection of them is the reconciling of the world, what would their acceptance be, but life from the dead? If the first fruit is holy, so is the lump. If the root is holy, so are the branches. But if some of the branches were broken off, and you, being a wild olive, were grafted in among them, and became partaker with them of the root and of the richness of the olive tree; don't boast over the branches. But if you boast, it is not you who support the root, but the root supports you. You will say then, "Branches were broken off, that I might be grafted in." True; by their unbelief, they were broken off, and you stand by your faith. Don't be conceited, but fear; for if God didn't spare the natural branches, neither will he spare you." (Romans 11:13-21)

Chapter 11 of Hebrews is often subtitled, *Heroes of the Faith* It goes on and on about how people that put their faith in God are commended, but the last two sentences are pretty interesting:

And all these, though commended through their faith, did not receive what was promised, since God had provided something better for us, that apart from us they should not be made perfect. (Hebrews 11:39-40 ESV)

That something better is His son, Jesus. In Him, all the promises of God are made complete.

It is the grafting of the non-Hebrews into the root and the adoption of believers in Christ that extend all the promises of Israel to all believers. All the promises to Israel in the Old Testament are applicable to each one of us today.

We often talk about the love of God and what he had done for us. But Hosea's story truly demonstrates the lengths that God has gone through to be in a relationship with each and every one of us. God uses Hosea's life as an example of how deep His love for us is. Right there in the second verse, God sets up the parallels between Hosea's relationship between himself and his family and God's relationship with his chosen people, Israel.

"When Yahweh spoke at first by Hosea, Yahweh said to Hosea, "Go, take for yourself a wife of prostitution and children of unfaithfulness; for the land commits great adultery, forsaking Yahweh." (Hosea 1:2)

Hosea's choice for a wife is Gomer. The best information I can find about her is that she was involved in the ritual sex acts in Baal cult worship. Some commentators say she was a prostitute. Others aren't so sure, but it is pretty much agreed that she was an immoral woman.

By Hosea's time, Baalism had recaptured the minds and hearts of many Israelites. Baal's followers believed that his blessing insured the continuation of human life and the preservation of social order. As a fertility deity, Baal was the provider of children, a prized possession in the culture of the Middle East. The reason Baalism was so successful was that the Lord demanded obedience to strict moral and ethical standards as the basis for a blessing. In stark contrast, Baalism appealed to the sensual nature. Baal's favor was gained through sympathetic magic in the form of ritual prostitution. Through these rites, young men and women supposedly could gain

Baal's favor and ensure their ability to produce and bear children. Because of Baalism's attractions to the base side of human nature, it persisted in Israel. It promised an easy and even enjoyable road to prosperity, while God's way, the way of true life, demanded selflessness.

Baalism succeeds because it promises us everything we want by appealing to our most sensual appetites. That's how the devil works, isn't it? Take something beautiful that God has given us, and perverts it into something ugly.

I like the way Screwtape explains this concept to Wormwood in CS Lewis' classic novel, The Screwtape Letters.

> Never forget that when we are dealing with any pleasure in its healthy and normal and satisfying form, we are, in a sense, on the Enemy's ground. I know we have won many a soul through pleasure. All the same, it is His invention, not ours. He made the pleasures: all our research so far has not enabled us to produce one. All we can do is to encourage the humans to take the pleasures which our Enemy has produced, at times, or in ways, or in degrees, which He has forbidden. Hence we always try to work away from the natural condition of any pleasure to that in which it is least natural, least redolent of its Maker, and least pleasurable. An ever increasing craving for an ever diminishing pleasure is the formula. It is more certain, and it's better style. To get the man's soul and give him nothing in return—that is what really gladdens our Father's heart. –C.S. Lewis, Screwtape Letters, chapter 9.

In this manner, God is using the example of Hosea and Gomer's marriage as an analogy of His relationship to each of us. He tells Hosea to take Gomer, a woman of whoredom and tells us that not only will her relationship to him be an analogy of God's relationship to Israel, but also her children because the Israelites have committed prostitution in their relationship with the LORD by bowing down to other gods.

Let's look at that statement before we go on. It seems incredibly harsh. One thing about the Old Testament is that God pretty much tells it like it is to the ones He loves. But even in the New Testament Jesus teaches that just physical observance of the Law is meaningless. We all know some if not all of the 10 commandments. We think that it's not all that hard to follow them, they are just basic rules for living, right? We understand not murdering someone, or stealing from them, right? In Jesus' Sermon on the Mount, He teaches that physical observance of the Law isn't the point of it at all, it's keeping our hearts and our minds pure. The two verses that relate to Hosea and Israel's situation is in Mark 5:27-28

> "You have heard that it was said, 'You shall not commit adultery.' But I say to you that everyone who looks at a woman with lustful intent has already committed adultery with her in his heart. (Mathew 5:27-28 ESV)

Adultery isn't merely a physical act between people that aren't married to each other; it's a state of our heart. Adultery involves a multitude of other acts including deceit and coveting, but more treacherous it robs the one we love of our total devotion. When we look at someone other than the one we love and even consider it, we have committed adultery in our hearts. And so it is with our relationship to God.

> "You shall have no other gods before me. "You shall not make for yourselves an idol, nor any image of anything that is in the heavens above, or that is in the earth beneath, or that is in the water under the earth: you shall not bow yourself down to them, nor serve them, for I, Yahweh your God, am a jealous God, visiting the iniquity of the fathers on the children, on the third and on the fourth generation of those who hate me," (Exodus 20:3-5)

How many times do we commit adultery against God when we look up our horoscopes or have our little luck charms? Play our lucky lotto numbers? The Bible doesn't directly speak to the issue of gambling, but if you know any gamblers, you know that they are a very superstitious bunch! Or how about athletes that have their lucky shorts or socks or shoes? How many of us professing Christians, those of us who claim to have our faith in Christ Himself, have our own little prayer angels or other things for good luck?

It's interesting to note that God commands Hosea to take a wife of whoredom. He commands Hosea to take a bride that is less than pure, less than clean. How does that relate to each of us? With all our imperfections, faults, and the bad things we do, God still wants to enter into the most intimate of relationships with each of us, as intimate as a man and a woman marrying.

The first child that comes in their marriage is Jezreel.

"So he went and took Gomer the daughter of Diblaim, and she conceived, and bore him a son." (Hosea 1:3)

She bore HIM a son. The marriage starts off well enough. But the paternity of the second child is questioned.

"She conceived again and bore a daughter. Then he said to him, "Call her name Lo-Ruhamah; for I will no longer have mercy on the house of Israel, that I should in any way pardon them." (Hosea 1:6)

Thus the scandal begins in the house of Hosea. The Scripture suggests that Lo-Ruhamah isn't Hoesa's child. Indirectly it says that "she bore a daughter," not "bore him a daughter." This isn't me just splitting hairs. The implication is further made by the name of the daughter, Lo-Ruhamah. The name literally means, "never knew a father's pity." God is saying to the people that have sunk into idolatry, "You will not know My pity for I am not your Father."

The next child there is no doubt that he isn't Hosea's child. The scripture reads:

> "Now when she had weaned Lo-Ruhamah, she conceived and bore a son. He said, "Call his name Lo-Ammi; for you are not my people, and I will not be yours." (Hosea 1:8-9)

Lo-Ammi literally means, "not my people," and if you apply it to a single individual, "not my child."

Thinking about Hosea. Hosea's love is Gomer, a prostitute in the Canaanite temples. God commanded him to marry her. Then after they were married, she was unfaithful. How many times are we unfaithful to God after He saves us over and over again? How many times do we bow down to Baal?

And then, as if that isn't bad enough, she leaves him because she wants finer things and thinks Hosea can't provide them. She ends up desperate and ends up selling herself into slavery. Hosea buys her out. The analogy is God's relationship with us that we are unfaithful to Him, but He never gives up on us.

Hosea is pretty hardcore. Of the 14 chapters, 13 of them deal with how badly Gomer and Israel treat Hosea and God. It truly demonstrates heartbreak on the part of God. It's not all bad news, however, because repeatedly throughout it mentions the promises of God to Israel. The final chapter starts out, "Return, O Israel, to the Lord your God." The final chapter of Hosea doesn't read about the wrath of God or the punishment of Israel. It's a pleading from God for us to return to Him. It's almost as if God is begging us to return. He in effect says, "Please come back home. I love you and will do great things for you if you do."

My favorite story in the Bible is the one of the prodigal son. Luke 15:20 is my favorite verse in the entire Bible:

"He arose and came to his father. But while he was still far off, his father saw him, and was moved with compassion, and ran, and fell on his neck, and kissed him." (Luke 15:20)

Return, O Israel, to the Lord your God. Let's talk about returning to the Lord our God. In the last couple of decades or so I've gotten 3 tickets for driving without insurance. Each time I had some excuse about why I didn't have insurance: couldn't afford it, didn't have time to pay the bill and was going to do it, or some equally ignorant excuse. The ticket for not having insurance then was $150 dollars, about what I pay for a month of insurance now. I carry insurance on my car now, but probably only because I am required to have it for my work. They tend to keep track of when my insurance expires and hold my paycheck until I am fully insured again.

Not carrying liability insurance on my car is against the law. I break the law every time I don't have the coverage the law requires. I know I should do it. I know it's the right thing to do. But unless I have someone watching me, I don't seem to think it's all that important.

It's like that with God's Law. We know we should do it, we know it's the right thing to do, but unless we have someone watching us, we often don't think it's all that important.

"Repent" and "repentance" are words that people throw at others to try to coerce them to do what they should be doing anyway. They talk about how you can't really be saved unless you repent and turn away from your sins. That just sounds like religious talk to me. My grace force field goes up when folks start talking about repenting I usually go into full grace mode and accuse them of trying to put me under that Law again!

But the fact of the matter is that Jesus told us to repent.

"From that time, Jesus began to preach, and to say, "Repent! For the Kingdom of Heaven is at hand." (Matthew 4:17)

In 5 of the 7 letters to the 7 churches in the Book of Revelations Jesus commands them to repent.

So what is *repentance* and how does one *repent*. I pretty much believe if you are asking that question, you probably are already on your way to doing it. Repentance is a fancy religious word that basically means "to turn away; to change one's mind." If one is asking how to do it, one is more than likely already in the process of changing their mind about something.

The Bible is full of useful information about how we are to act and behave and what God expects of us. People that like to tell us to repent usually are trying to force us into behaving a particular way lest we are condemned to hell for eternity. However, Jesus did not come to condemn the world; He came to save it.

> "For God did not send the Son into the world to judge the world, but that the world might be saved through Him. (John 3:17 NASB)

He came in order that we should not suffer the fate of eternal damnation.

> "I have not come to call the righteous, but sinners to repentance." (Luke 5:32)

Paul writes about repentance when he says that we should no longer conform to this world but be transformed by the renewal of our minds.[25]

I had been meditating on this whole repentance thing for a few weeks. I kept thinking there was a connection between repentance and the *Lord's Supper*, but couldn't really figure out what it was. Over and over in my head, I heard, "the life is in the blood." Finally while crossing a 2-mile bridge over a lake, it came to me. Repentance is when we finally accept the blood

---

25 Romans 12:2

of Christ. When we take communion, we are merely acknowledging what has happened in our minds and hearts.

Unlike my auto insurance which I have, because I fear the State of Texas and my employer when I don't have it, repentance is when I turn to God because I want to turn to Him, not because I fear the consequences.

> There is no fear in love; but perfect love casts out fear, because fear involves punishment, and the one who fears is not perfected in love. (1 John 4:18 NASB)

"Love covers a multitude of sins" (1 Pet 4:8), but at some point, you don't want to have to be covered all the time, you want to do what is right. You want to stop sinning against God. You know that He will forgive you, but you want to give Him less to forgive. That is repentance.

Often (okay, almost all the time), God lets us suffer in our sins until we turn from them. As we grow in relationship to Him, we often feel bad when we know we've let him down. The Bible tells us:

> "I now rejoice, not that you were made sorry, but that you were made sorry to repentance. For you were made sorry in a godly way, that you might suffer loss by us in nothing. For godly sorrow produces repentance to salvation, which brings no regret. But the sorrow of the world produces death." (2 Corinthians 7:9-10)

I wrote extensively about that God loves unconditionally and that grace forgives repeatedly.[26] Peter writes:

> "The Lord is not slow concerning his promise, as some count slowness; but is patient with us, not wishing that any should perish, but that all should come to repentance." (2 Peter 3:9)

---

26 1 Corinthians 13:7

The patience of the Lord astounds me.

The Bible is the story of our spiritual journey. It is God's love letter to us. In it, we learn of our wonderful creation. We read that we began in the garden with God, but then we were unfaithful to Him, and we had to leave. As we go on through the Bible, we read of our trials and tribulations, of God's yearning to reconcile us to Him. God wants us. He loves us. We all know John 3:16, *For God so loved the world that He gave his only begotten son, that whosoever believes in Him shall not perish but have everlasting life.* Because of the promises to Israel, God had to sacrifice His only Son. That sacrifice bought each of us out of prison and made us presentable to God.

> he has now reconciled in his body of flesh by his death, in order to present you holy and blameless and above reproach before him, (Colossians 1:22 ESV)

THAT is how much God loves you. He goes after us regardless of what we do. He does anything it takes to make us presentable to us. Jesus said

> Greater love has no one than this that someone lay down his life for his friends. (John 15:13 ESV)

Just as Hosea pursued Gomer, God pursues us. The crux of God's desire is to have the most intimate relationship possible with each and every one of us. The type of relationship that can only come in a marriage environment. In the Revelation, John describes the relationship in that exact way.

> "I saw a new heaven and a new earth: for the first heaven and the first earth have passed away, and the sea is no more. I saw the holy city, New Jerusalem, coming down out of heaven from God, prepared like a bride adorned

for her husband. I heard a loud voice out of heaven saying, "Behold, God's dwelling is with people, and he will dwell with them, and they will be his people, and God himself will be with them as their God. He will wipe away every tear from their eyes. Death will be no more; neither will there be mourning, nor crying, nor pain, any more. The first things have passed away." (Revelation 21:1-4)

Chapter Fifteen
Stealing My Joy

There is no shortage of people willing to attempt to "steal my joy." What disturbs me the most is when those people are my brothers and sisters in Christ. I've waxed poetic in prior writings about religion and denominations and the lack of unity in the body of Christ, but today while my children were decorating our Christmas Tree, an old demon whispered into the back of my mind, "Don't put up a Christmas tree, it's against the Bible!" Thoughts like this come up every "Christian" holiday. Not specifically the tree thing, but that our (Christian) observance of the holiday is somehow actually some sort of pagan or even satanic ritual.

There is some truth to all of this, of course. Even myths are based upon something. The church in Rome did coopt many pagan observances and "Christianize" them. A lot of this co-opting came about when Christianity became the state religion of Rome. Nicene Christianity became the state church of the Roman Empire with the Edict of Thessalonica in 380 AD when Emperor Theodosius I made it the Empire's sole authorized religion. Rome's *modus operandi* was to conquer a nation and then bring the local customs and culture into the Roman customs and cultures. With Christianity being the official religion, Rome went into a community and adopted all the local religious observances and made them "Christian," thereby making the people converts. A book that details how much the church in Rome adopted a pagan religion and its practices is *The Two Babylons* written by Scottish theologian Alexander Hislop and published in 1853. I should note that Alexander Hislop was a Presbyterian theologian so let it be noted he was biased against Roman Catholicism from the start. The book details Hislop's theories of how the Babylonian mystery religion invaded the Roman Catholic Church. It's a convincing read, and there wasn't any real scholarly challenge to it until 2011.

My own thinking regarding many of these Christianized pagan holidays has changed since my youth. Growing up my family were Christians in name only. We didn't go to church. We didn't read the Bible. We didn't pray. We didn't have Scriptures on our refrigerator. You get the idea. My mom tells me now that we had a set of illustrated Bible stories and I vaguely remember them. We had only secular observances of the major Christian holidays Easter and Christmas. Those were really the only two days God or Jesus was mentioned in our home. I now find it amusing that the "proper way to observe Easter is to eat an unclean animal." As I began my journey as a Christian, those 2 holidays took on significantly more meaning. Easter became *the* holiday to celebrate. What could be more important than the day we celebrate our Savior rising from the dead and redeeming us?

As my relationship with God *deepened*, I became cynical of both of those holidays because of the secular and commercial influences that have overtaken both. I fail to see how Santa Claus, elves, toys, or tinsel has to do with the birth of the Savoir. Growing up I heard Christmas was for the children or Christmas was for families. The only actual explanation I received that Christmas had anything to do with the birth of Jesus was *A Charlie Brown Christmas* and some of the songs we sang like *Away In A Manger* and *Silent Night*. Cynicism aside, however, I can celebrate *any day* to God, and I can enjoy secular events as well (most Christians I know don't have issues with Independence Day or Veteran's Day, etc.). I also love my parents, and if they want to give presents to my kids or myself, I'm gracious enough to accept them!

When I learned about the *Feasts of the Lord* (Leviticus 23) and how they are intended to both teach us about God's plan for mankind and for us to *practice* for those plans, I became even more uninterested in secular observances. I personally believe now that Jesus was born during the Feast of Tabernacles (Sukkot) which occurs on our calendar around the third week in September and that the resurrection happened on the first day of the Feast of First Fruits following Passover. Sukkot will never happen on December 25th, and First Fruits rarely coincides with Easter (2017 a notable exception).

That said, the source of all these thoughts that our observance of any event is demonic in nature usually comes from people that somehow think they have some sort of superiority over me and are much more enlightened than I am.

During Easter the discussion always comes around to Ishtar, at Christmas time, the discussion centers on the fact that there is no evidence the early church celebrated the birth of the Savior and that the holiday is, in fact, a man-made "Christianization" of a pagan holiday (Winter Solstice). Furthermore, and the point I want to focus upon, that it is unbiblical to put up and decorate a Christmas tree.

Like nearly all good lies, the concept of it being unbiblical to put up a Christmas tree is found in some truth.

> "Hear the word which Yahweh speaks to you, house of Israel! Yahweh says, "Don't learn the way of the nations, and don't be dismayed at the signs of the sky; for the nations are dismayed at them. For the customs of the peoples are vanity; for one cuts a tree out of the forest, the work of the hands of the workman with the ax. They deck it with silver and with gold. They fasten it with nails and with hammers so that it can't move. They are like a palm tree, of turned work, and don't speak. They must be carried because they can't move. Don't be afraid of them; for they can't do evil, neither is it in them to do good." (Jeremiah 10:1-5)

That certainly appears at first glance to be referring to Christmas trees. The passage describes using an ax on a tree and putting tinsel on it (okay, it actually says "deck it with silver

and gold" but I can read in between the lines well as the next
armchair theologian!) The problem with that doctrine is that
Verse 3 in the ESV reads …worked with an axe by the hands
of a craftsman, and in the NASB verse 3 reads …worked by
the hands of a craftsman with a cutting tool. This passage is
clearly speaking directly to making idols and idol worship. The
passage says "they fasten it with nails and with hammers so
that it can't move. They are like a palm tree, of turned work,
and don't speak." This is a direct reference to idol worship.

> "There you shall serve gods, the work of men's hands,
> wood and stone, which neither see, nor hear, nor eat, nor
> smell." (Deuteronomy 4:28)

I think the argument here could be better made that this
passage of Scripture (Jeremiah 10:1-5) addresses all the ornate
crosses and that we use to decorate our homes and churches.

How many of us have prayed to our Christmas tree
compared to those of us that have prayed to a cross (kneeling
at the foot of a cross or holding one in our closed hands)
thinking that somehow that made our prayers better heard?

Just for the record, I have never prayed to a Christmas tree
nor have I ever intentionally prayed to a cross. Holding up a
cross as a sign just as Moses held up the snake in the wilderness
is another chapter for another time (although what Jesus said
is "And just as Moses lifted up the serpent in the wilderness,
so must the Son of Man be lifted up, that whoever believes in
him may have eternal life." John 3:14-15).

When it comes to celebrating Christmas, I look to what
Paul wrote about religious observances.

> "One man esteems one day as more important. Another
> esteems every day alike. Let each man be fully assured in
> his own mind. He who observes the day, observes it to
> the Lord; and he who does not observe the day, to the
> Lord he does not observe it. He who eats, eats to the
> Lord, for he gives God thanks. He who doesn't eat, to

the Lord he doesn't eat and gives God thanks. For none of us lives to himself, and none dies to himself. For if we live, we live to the Lord. Or if we die, we die to the Lord. If therefore we live or die, we are the Lord's. For to this end, Christ died, rose, and lived again, that he might be Lord of both the dead and the living. But you, why do you judge your brother? Or you again, why do you despise your brother? For we will all stand before the judgment seat of Christ. For it is written, "'As I live,' says the Lord, 'to me every knee will bow. Every tongue will confess to God.'" (Romans 14:5-11)

Many of those that would bind us with legalistic requirements to not observe a religious observance do so because "they" know the true origin of the practice and that "it" is really a pagan or satanic ritual that we Christians have been deceived into worshiping someone other than Christ. I would submit that attitude demonstrates a "spirit of religion." It's self-righteousness for sure to be superior to your fellow believers because you have a correct doctrine or theology. However, the Bible teaches us that God knows the heart and mind of a man.

"But Yahweh said to Samuel, "Don't look on his face, or on the height of his stature, because I have rejected him; for I don't see as man sees. For man looks at the outward appearance, but Yahweh looks at the heart." (1 Samuel 16:7)

"then hear in heaven, your dwelling place, and forgive, and act, and give to every man according to all his ways, whose heart you know (for you, even you only, know the hearts of all the children of men);" (1 Kings 8:39)

"then hear from heaven your dwelling place and forgive, and render to every man according to all his ways, whose heart you know (for you, even you only, know the hearts of the children of men)" (2 Chronicles 6:30)

God knows what is in our heart, no matter what the external actions may look like. The one who observes the day, observes it in honor of the Lord. The one who eats, eats in honor of the Lord, since he gives thanks to God, while the one who abstains, abstains in honor of the Lord and gives thanks to God.

"for when Gentiles who don't have the law do by nature the things of the law, these, not having the law, are a law to themselves," (Romans 2:14)

Chapter Sixteen
A Drink Of Water

A few years back the church I attended was meeting every Sunday night to watch and discuss a video series called H20. The very first night the video we watched addressed the story in the book of John of the Samaritan woman at the well. This short passage is the one where Jesus says to the woman, "Whoever drinks of this water will thirst again, but whoever drinks the water that I shall give him will never thirst."

During the course of the discussion, Rachel asked the question, "If Jesus is the living water and whoever drinks of it will never be thirsty again, why do so many Christians come to church thirsty every week?" That question really gets to the point of the entire H20 video series. It's designed to get us asking questions and then to dwell on spiritual things. I know it's a deep question because 5 weeks later people in the congregation were still talking about it. Each week during the discussion people in one regard or another attempted to answer that or a variation of that question. It's a hard question.

In the Pirates of the Caribbean movies, there is a reference to an island you can only find if you already know where it is. What we will discover is we already know the answer to Rachel's question. I'm going to approach the question in two different ways. First, break down the passage that sparked this question, and then directly address it. First, let's read the passage together. It's in the book of John, chapter 4, verses 10-15

Jesus answered and said to her, "If you knew the gift of God, and who it is who says to you, 'Give Me a drink,' you would have asked Him, and He would have given you living water." The woman said to Him, "Sir, You have nothing to draw with, and the well is deep. Where then do You get that living water? Are You greater than our father Jacob, who gave us the well, and drank from it himself, as well as his sons and his livestock?" Jesus answered and said to her, "Whoever drinks of this water will thirst again, but whoever drinks of the water that I shall give him will never thirst. But the water that I shall give him will become in him a fountain of water springing up into everlasting life." The woman said to Him, "Sir, give me this water, that I may not thirst, nor come here to draw."

If this is true, why do so many of us who claim to be Christians, those of us who claim to know of the Risen Lord Jesus Christ, those of us that are pretty sure that at least one time we've drunk this living water, why is it that so many of us are THIRSTY? Before I tell you what I think the answer is, let me ask you a question:

Do you have a Bible in your home?

I'm pretty sure every one of us has a Bible or at least access to one. The next question:

How many of us spent at a minimum one-hour this week outside of church reading our Bible?

Or Praying?

Or singing praises to God?

Or maybe an hour total of those three activities combined?

These are the types of questions I can write out but couldn't really ask in church for a show of hands!

How many of us watched at least an episode of "Duck Dynasty" or "X-Factor" or "The Bachelor" or "Dancing with the Stars" or some other reality show this week? Isn't each episode an hour long? What does that say about us if we can watch one or more hours of television a week but we don't have an hour to spend with God outside of church? Now I'm not picking on you or any of these shows. Monday night while you were watching Dancing with the Stars I was bowling, and bowling takes longer than an hour; it's a 3-hour commitment. Tuesday night during Idol I was playing bass working on music for the following weeks' service. I don't include that time as "singing to God" or worship or anything like that because when we work on arrangements, it's all about performance and not worship. The point is that we have time for what is important to us. We all have to make choices about what to do with our time. We spend that time with whoever we think is important enough to spend our time with. We chose to spend time bowling or watching TV or to spend time with God.

Look again at the verses we looked at earlier, particularly the second part of verse 14: "but whoever drinks of the water that I shall give him will never thirst. But the water that I shall give him will become in him a fountain of water springing up into everlasting life." As Christians, we have all tasted the living water of God. We all have had those moments where we have tasted and seen that He is good.

What we are missing from this passage of Scripture is that *the woman had to go to the well every day to draw water*. When she was thirsty, she had to go to the well. Jesus tells us that when He gives us living water, He puts the water in us. The point He makes isn't that we get one drink of water and are never thirsty again. If that were the case, we'd get saved and be done. Go to the house. Sit around and wait for the rapture, right? Instead, when we drink the water, He places the well deep down inside us. We don't have to go to the well; it is already here. The Lord is right here, right now. The reason we never have to thirst again is that the well is right there right now. We who are thirsty are like the little Dutch boy that put his finger in the dike to stop the flow of water. Inside each and every one of us is a fountain of water springing up into everlasting life!

Chapter Seventeen
First Encounter

My first encounter with religion occurred sometime around second grade circa 1974. Being that I was only 6 or 7 at the time this event happened the exact date eludes me, but the memory of that experience is etched into my mind as if it happened only a couple of years ago. It's quite possible that things that actually did happen two years ago have been totally forgotten but only because my brain can only hold so many memories and this one won't let go.

My father had finished his tours of duty in the Vietnam War and was stateside once again. His new assignment was a little less graphic; he was assigned as an army recruiter in Cedar Rapids, Iowa, so that's where he, my mother, my brother, and I moved. My parents even bought a house there. Cedar Rapids left a pretty good impression on me because even at that young age I have a lot of really fond memories from there. One example: people are always impressed that Jesus and Peter walked on water. When the subject comes up, I can honestly say I have also walked on water. Seriously. I did it on the Cedar River. Really. Of course, the water was frozen when I did it, but I walked on water, and no one can deny it! Another thing I remember fondly was this was the only time in my life that I actually walked to school. After we left Iowa, I rode a bus for the rest of my school career.

This first encounter happened with my brother, as we were walking home from school. Since my brother was with me, it must have been second grade because he's 2 years my junior. A local church had some event going on for a couple weeks, and they'd have kids come from a school for typical vacation bible school type adventures, and then after that, there was some sort of church service. David and I never went to the church service, we just did our crafts, ate cookies and then walked home. This particular day was different though because as we were walking through the sanctuary to leave, I noticed them. Drums. Yes, *DRUMS!* What I am about to convey to you is the direct result of a small boy's fascination with something he'd never actually seen in real life. I had already declared to everyone in the second grade that when I grow up, I'm going to be a rock and roll singer! *Cool* is all I thought. I was fascinated with them. I don't remember what I said, but I do remember talking to the guy setting up the drums and waxing poetic about my love for them. I was talking to this guy with some seriously long hair and beard, a tee shirt and jeans. He must have been one of the Jesus Freaks of the 70's because I remember his appearance exactly like the stereotypical hippie of the time. Alas, my brother and I couldn't stay because we didn't have permission to stay after the craft part of whatever they were doing. David and I went home, but when we got home, I was still going on and on about those drums. Pretty sure based on how my 4 years old lets me know that she wants something that my mom agreed that my brother and I could stay later the next day just so I'd stop talking.

The next day after school David and I practically ran to the church and into the sanctuary to make sure the drums were still there. They were! I was excited. I could hardly stand to wait through the usual stuff we did after school. Finally, the time for the service arrived. *Oh Boy!* They did not let me down either. The band came out and performed several songs. The drums were *awesome* even though I'm pretty sure I didn't use that word when I was 7.

Things shifted after the band finished playing. I was still drumming in my mind as the speaker began to deliver his sermon. *FIRE AND WORMS THAT DIETH NOT AND I'M GOING TO HELL* went on for what seemed an eternity. I had never heard such talk in my life. We didn't go to church, we just came and did crafts after school and ate cookies. *I just wanted to see and hear the drums!* THEY TRICKED ME! On and on he went on about these worms not dying and burning in hell if we don't ask Jesus to be our Lord and Savior and make sure we go to heaven and not to hell. My 7-year-old mind didn't have a lot of life experience to go on, but I was pretty sure I didn't want to go to hell and be a roasted treat for worms that never die.

I didn't know what he was talking about at the time, but just for reference, this is the Scripture, and I'm pretty sure the translation he was preaching out of:

> "And whosoever shall offend one of these little ones that believe in me; it is better for him that a millstone were hanged about his neck, and he were cast into the sea. And if thy hand offend thee, cut it off: it is better for thee to enter into life maimed than having two hands to go into hell, into the fire that never shall be quenched: Where their worm dieth not, and the fire is not quenched. And if thy foot offends thee, cut it off: it is better for thee to enter halt into life than having two feet to be cast into hell, into the fire that never shall be quenched: Where their worm dieth not, and the fire is not quenched. And if thine eye offends thee, pluck it out: it is better for thee to enter into the kingdom of God with one eye than having two eyes to be cast into hell fire: Where their worm dieth not, and the fire is not quenched." (Mark 9:42-48, KJV)

Petrified, I sat there as the preacher made the altar call. As soon as he did my younger brother shot down to the front to ask Jesus to save him. I couldn't move. Literally. I didn't want to go to hell, and I certainly was not interested in being eaten by worms that dieth not, but I was so shocked by what I had heard that I couldn't move. I sat there helpless and doomed and cried because I couldn't join what seemed like every single other person in the room down front at the altar. Everyone else managed to run down there, and they just left me there to burn in hell and get eaten by worms.

Finally, it was over. Somehow we managed to walk home. I was not my usual self. I was quiet. Consumed with the fact that I was going to die and go to hell and be roasted worm food. Over and over in my mind, I heard the preacher, "AND THE WORM DIETH NOT!" Over and over.

David and I shared a room so at bedtime after the good nights and lights out I asked him why he ran down to the front. He said he didn't know; he just knew he didn't want to die and go to hell. I told him I didn't want to do that either. I asked him what they did on the altar. He told me the preacher had him say a prayer saying that he was a worthless sinner and asking Jesus to be his Lord and Savior and save him from hell. I thought about that as I heard that evangelist talk about fire and worms repeatedly in my head. I didn't want to go to hell and saying some words seemed easy enough for me so in the middle of the night when I wasn't sleeping anyway, I got out of my bed, kneeled down on the floor and said the prayer.

I really wish I could tell you that at that moment I had an encounter with God right there in my bedroom in the middle of that night, heard the angelic choir and it changed my life forever. Really, I *wish* I could tell you all that, but the very best I could have hoped for is that I might have gotten some fire insurance.

To this day I relive this memory every time I see some really young kids (just for the sake of quantifying this, let's say 9 years and under) come forward in a service to get saved. They say the prayer and everyone applauds and tells them the angels are dancing in heaven for them. For most of them, this is a great day and a positive memory.

I don't know if I was truly saved that day or not. I was told I was saved and for years if anyone asked, I told them I was. However, I really had no concept of what that meant. I had no concept of being born again and certainly had no clue who I had prayed to so as not to go to hell.

My brother and I never went back to the afterschool program at that church. It was a really long time before I even considered anything religious or church-related again.

Years later, just as I was going to into high school, my father retired from the army after 24 years of service and our family moved to Lufkin, Texas. Seemed like an odd place to go to retire. Dad was from Lufkin, but he didn't seem to have a particular fondness for the place and even told me this about his enlistment:

> *My brother and I got into some trouble at the Pines Theater downtown. We got picked up by the sheriff, and the sheriff told me I had one of two choices; jail or the army.*

If I am to believe my dad, the sheriff literally drove him to the recruiter's office and watched him and his brother enlist. I think he came to like the order and the discipline the military provided. It was a complete one-eighty of the chaos that had been his childhood. His parents were both alcoholics and divorced when he was only 4 years old, and his brother and two sisters have bounced around from aunt and uncle to grandparent to whoever would take them. The children were separated and didn't really ever live together. I've only met my two aunts once when I was in junior high school. I asked him once why he came back to Lufkin because I couldn't understand why he'd go to the place that has so many negative memories for him. All he told me was that after moving us (my brother and I) every 18-24 months our entire life it was time to put down some roots somewhere and he didn't really have any other place to call home. With his experience in the army he could have made significantly more money at his second career out on either coast of the United States or even in Europe, but he sacrificed that to be able to come home after 5:00 PM and be home on the weekends. By the time he retired, I also had a sister and another brother. I have absolutely no memories of ever doing anything with my father prior to his retirement and us moving to Texas.

So we moved to Lufkin, Texas. My dad went to work as the foreman of the truck shop of the fiberboard plant at Temple-Inland in Diboll (about 20 miles from where we lived), and my parents bought a house in the Hudson community. I started 9th grade in the Lufkin Independent School District. At that time, the 8th and 9th grades were the junior high school so technically, while I was a freshman, I was still in the junior high school. I couldn't really tell any major difference between that junior high and the one I had just left. By the end of the first grading period, we moved to our family home that my mom still lives in Hudson.

Hudson High School was a complete culture shock to me. Lufkin school seemed just like the last school I attended in Leesville, Louisiana, while my dad served his final military assignment at Fort Polk. Hudson, however, was *different*. For one thing, the entire school district was on one campus. My entire class only had 92 people in it. They had something called FFA that I had no concept of what that might be (you probably know, but for the one person that doesn't, Future Farmers of America), but the one thing that just blew my mind was every single morning someone came on the intercom and *prayed*. Not only did someone pray, but they also prayed to the Lord Jesus Christ in His name! They didn't even bother to keep it a generic prayer to some generic deity. This was 1980, and it was a pretty rare thing to hear prayer in school over the public address system. It was rare enough that I hadn't ever heard it done before in my 14 years on earth.

People were friendly enough. I found it odd that one of the very first questions I was asked over and over again by everyone is, "what religion are you?" That was curious because I'd lived in a dozen other places in my short lifetime and I couldn't ever remember getting asked that question. All I knew was on my dog tag it said my religion was "Protestant." Since we never went to church, I just knew about Catholics, Protestants, and Jews. I'd seen those buildings on the military bases I'd lived at. I had never heard of Jehovah's Witnesses or Pentecostals or Mormons, or Baptists, or Methodists, etc. So I answered the question the only way I knew how that I'm a Protestant. "What's that?" I got asked over and over again. I didn't know. It's just what it said on my dog tag. I was telling my dad about this dilemma, and he told me just to tell people I was a Baptist, and they'd be happy about that.

That satisfied me, and for weeks I would tell people I was a Baptist, and I came to find out most of them were too, so that was a good thing. What my dad neglected to tell me about Baptists is that they really value membership in their churches and they are very evangelical in nature. So once all the Baptists found out I was a "Baptist," they needed to know which Baptist church I was a member. I'm pretty convinced in Hudson, Texas, in 1989 there were 3 Baptist churches for every single man, woman, child, and dog. When I would tell them I didn't go to church, I suddenly found out I was everyone's mission. Every Saturday, while I was washing my car the youth pastors and groups from multiple churches, would begin to visit me one after another. Literally. I think they got together and worked out a schedule. One group would be leaving as another was pulling into my driveway. I've heard every single evangelical script created in the 1980's. I have the Roman's Road memorized. I got asked over and over again if I died tonight do I know what would happen? That was one of the easier questions because I knew I had said the sinner's prayer in my bedroom in Cedar Rapids Iowa so that I would go to heaven and not to hell. When I told them I'd said the sinner's prayer, and they confirmed I'd said the correct words, they would be satisfied for a while, but they still needed me to come to their church "just one time." I found out later that most of these groups kept score. Some of the churches I ended up visiting had the scoreboard up in the sanctuary!

I wish I could tell you that during my high school years I started going to church and had an encounter with God that changed me forever, but I didn't. I did attend one church for about a year. I learned a lot of doctrines and got my first taste of end times theology. I learned a lot of rules and what I couldn't do. The one thing I didn't find was a relationship with

Jesus Christ. God was still some mythical guy "up there" that had a bunch of rules and regulations (seriously, read Leviticus sometime!) and was going to send me to hell if I didn't ask his son to be my Lord.

By my junior year in high school, I pretty much quit the whole church thing. The little church I had been attending quit appealing to me because the sermon was the same every week: you need to get saved so we can put another number up on the board. Week after week the sermon was how I needed to get saved. Okay, I'm saved. I said the prayer. Now what? There wasn't anything after that.

It would be the year 2004, 30 years after my first encounter with religion, before I would have a genuine encounter with my Lord, Christ Jesus. What a glorious day that was! I consider myself fortunate that I didn't have to wander for 40 years as the Hebrews did in the desert.

Chapter Eighteen
Meeting Jesus Christ

In 1989 I got married, and my son was born. My wife and I didn't go to church and what little religion we had in our home was whatever Oprah was promoting at the time. (we seemed to pick and choose whatever was convenient for us). I didn't really give it any thought for years until my son was about to go into junior high school.

My son Zach was about to start high school. I started thinking about my own high school experience. All those youth groups came back to my mind. I told my wife that we needed to start teaching our children about God before some little renegade evangelist from a cult does it for us. She agreed, but the problem was neither of us knew anything about God either.

I knew I had to find a church for my family. I did not want a repeat of my Iowa experience for my children nor did I want week after week after week of soul winning and then nothing afterward. My wife agreed. She had had her own struggles with the church and was very specific that she would not go to a Southern Baptist church. Period. Do you have any idea how many Southern Baptist Churches there were in East Texas circa 1990-2000?

I fell in love with the guitar when I was 13 years old and had been playing ever since I got my first Sears & Roebuck guitar for Christmas that year. By the 90's I was playing and touring in bar bands and had my own PA system. About the time I was searching for a church for my family I was in the local music store. A couple of women came into the store looking to rent a PA System for their church Christmas program. The store did rent systems, but they didn't have any equipment available for the dates requested. The owner knew me; I was in the store hanging out when he suggested, "Danny has a PA, maybe he'll rent it to you."

I was introduced to Connie and Rebecca. While we were discussing their PA needs, I told them I was looking for a church. Naturally, they invited me to theirs. They found out I played bass (my main instrument since about 1992) and invited me to come to play with them in their program. I went home and told my wife that I was going to play in this church's Christmas program so we could check them out.

This was my introduction to the Unity Church of Christianity. We went to the first rehearsal at the church. It was a small group. In all the years we spent with them I don't recall more than 40 people ever coming to a single service. I remember a lot where the only ones there were the visiting preacher, the person who unlocked the door, and my family. At that first rehearsal for the Christmas program, my wife and I were looking through their library. They had an interesting collection of books. Everything from channeling and reincarnation to one book I found called "Jesus Christ Heals." Seemed weird but they were doing a Christmas Program, and they had the word "Christianity" in their name.

For six years we attended the Unity Church of Christianity. For all of those six years, I was told everything I was being taught was in the Bible. I wasn't really familiar with what was actually in the Bible at the time, but I found it odd how little we actually used the Bible in the teaching. Typically a single line of Scripture would be used to start a lesson/sermon, and then extraneous sources would be used to teach. Unity has 2 main books, "Lessons In Truth" and the "Metaphysical Bible Dictionary." The founders also authored numerous other books, and I'm pretty sure over time I read them all. I'm not here to call them a cult or be derogatory because honestly, in the years since I've been to plenty of churches where everything, but Christ seems to be the focus. The Unity Church of Christianity is a "new thought" church. I was in hook, line, and sinker, so to speak. I was actually getting funding together to go to their seminary right before we left.

It never seemed right to me to tell me that "everything we teach is from the Bible," but never hear anyone really teach or read from the Bible. I was training to be a pastor in the church, so I got to teach. Teach I did. I would take whatever I was supposed to teach about and then go find the Bible verses that would prove me right. I've since discovered that lots of people in lots of different religions or denominations do the same thing, decide what they want God to say and then find Scripture to back it up. I got really good at cherry-picking verses to prove my point. If verse one fit, verse two didn't, and verse three did again, I'd just leave the second one out when reading the Bible. Being totally ignorant about the Bible I actually was introduced as the resident "Rhodes Bible Scholar" by my pastor because when I would teach Unity Principles, I would always use a lot of Scripture to back it up, thus verifying what they were telling me, "everything we teach is in the Bible." I was a hero.

One day during my meditation, I had what might be my first real encounter with Jesus. I had a vision, and in the vision, He told me to "Read my book." The gravity of that statement didn't really fall on me until years later when my first Christian pastor would often say, "Read the Bible. You don't want to get to Heaven, meet Jesus, and the first question you ask Him He answers, 'That's in My book. You did read My book, didn't you?'" However, at that time the vision made sense to me because I'd been wondering what "our textbook" actually has to say about anything without it being filtered through the works of the founders of our church. What I was being taught and what I was teaching certainly did not match up with what I had been taught in the various Sunday school classes I attended while in high school.

I had literally no idea how to read and study the Bible. Every lesson/sermon I'd ever heard in my entire life seemed to cherry-pick verses to prove a point. For whatever reason, I'd never heard anyone teach/preach from a full passage of

Scripture. Being college educated, I decided to just read from page 1 to the end. I had a really nice Oxford Annotated New Revised Standard Version with notes in it. At the time Unity was partial to the NRSV, and to this day it's still my preferred translation (more on that later). So, one day I opened to Genesis 1:1 and started reading.

Within days I was consumed with reading the entire Bible. I was spending two to three hours a day reading page after page and the study notes in my Bible. I was amazed every time I read something like this:

> "In the same hour, the fingers of a man's hand came out and wrote near the lampstand on the plaster of the wall of the king's palace. The king saw the part of the hand that wrote." (Daniel 5:5)

And realizing it was talking about the "writing on the wall," an expression I knew but never knew came from the Bible. There were many others.

Most evangelist's scripts are taken from the New Testament, but my Damascus moment occurred while I was still in the Old one. It was the book of Isaiah. Early on in chapter 7, I recognized part of the Christmas story:

> "Therefore, the Lord himself will give you a sign. Behold, the virgin will conceive, and bear a son, and shall call his name Immanuel." (Isaiah 7:14)

I remember stopping at that verse and thinking, "that's Mary and Jesus!" Maybe I just remembered Linus' monolog in *A Charlie Brown Christmas;* maybe it was the Holy Spirit bringing all things into remembrance (John 14:26), I don't know. I do know that I SAW HIM in those verses. I was excited. I was happy. Finally, Jesus was real and not just some metaphysical concept in my mind.

I continued reading the Bible daily. Locked in a room away from my wife and children I read the Bible for hours at a

time. My real salvation moment occurred while reading Isaiah
53:

"Who has believed what we have heard? And to whom
has the arm of the LORD been revealed? For he grew
up before him like a young plant, and like a root out of
dry ground; he had no form or majesty that we should
look at him, nothing in his appearance that we should
desire him. He was despised and rejected by others; a
man of suffering and acquainted with infirmity; and as
one from whom others hide their faces he was despised,
and we held him of no account. Surely he has borne our
infirmities and carried our diseases; yet we accounted
him stricken, struck down by God, and afflicted. But he
was wounded for our transgressions, crushed for our
iniquities; upon him was the punishment that made us
whole, and by his bruises, we are healed. All we like
sheep have gone astray; we have all turned to our own
way, and the LORD has laid on him the iniquity of us
all. He was oppressed, and he was afflicted, yet he did
not open his mouth; like a lamb that is led to the
slaughter, and like a sheep that before its shearers are
silent, so he did not open his mouth. By a perversion of
justice, he was taken away. Who could have imagined his
future? For he was cut off from the land of the living,
stricken for the transgression of my people. They made
his grave with the wicked and his tomb with the rich,
although he had done no violence, and there was no
deceit in his mouth. Yet it was the will of the LORD to
crush him with pain. When you make his life an offering
for sin, he shall see his offspring, and shall prolong his
days; through him, the will of the LORD shall prosper.
Out of his anguish, he shall see light; he shall find
satisfaction through his knowledge. The righteous one,
my servant, shall make many righteous, and he shall bear
their iniquities. Therefore, I will allow him a portion with

the great, and he shall divide the spoil with the strong; because he poured out himself to death, and was numbered with the transgressors; yet he bore the sin of many, and made intercession for the transgressors." (Isaiah 53:1-12, NRSV)

I purposely used the NRSV here because I wanted to share with you exactly what I read. In this passage, everything I ever knew about Jesus and the Cross and the Crucifixion and Easter and the Resurrection came flooding into my mind. I was swimming in these words. I finally understood what God has done for me. I remember on this night, swimming in these words, I prayed, "Jesus, I don't know if I'm really saved or not, but You are God, and You died for my sins. Thank you. I don't know if I'll ever live up to Your expectations, but if You'll have me, I'm yours.

ABOUT THE AUTHOR

Danny Powell grew up in a secular home and didn't become a born-again believer until age 36. A harrowing experience he was totally unprepared for in a church when he was six years old caused it to take another 30 years to come face to face with Jesus. Since becoming a believer, Danny has shared his thoughts and observations in multiple blogs and has been a guest speaker at numerous churches and conference. In 2017 at the age of 51, he received ordination at the Healing Center of East Texas. Danny lives with his wife and his two youngest children in the oldest town in Texas, Nacogdoches.